A Time to Grieve

A Time to Grieve

Parent Grief for Handicapped Children

Ben N. Davidson

To order additional copies of this book, contact:
Xlibris Corporation
1-888-795-4274
www.Xlibris.com
Orders@Xlibris.com
59943

Contents

Dedicated

To Grace
Who makes me better than I am

Acknowledgments

To Grace, this book would never have been finished without your encouragement and faith. For over twenty-five years of pushing and shoving, I thank you. We finally got it done.

To my five great kids, you have been an inspiration. Your accomplishments and your lives have made me proud. I am proud to call you mine, and I am proud to be your dad.

To the many children that I have had the opportunity to work with over the past forty-one years, you have made me look good. Keep up the good work.

To the parents of the kids that I have worked with, thanks for sharing your child with me and allowing me to be a part of your lives. Your bravery in the face of tremendous problems inspired me daily. Keep the faith and grieve well.

Introduction

It has been my pleasure to work with handicapped children for over forty-one years. During that time, one of the most difficult areas of concern has been parent grief. Grief is natural and we, as professionals and parents, must be involved in that grief. Our preparedness to assist parents through the grief process is detrimental to our patient's recovery and their ability to live with their handicaps.

Life is full of ups and downs. Throughout our lives we are in a constant state of happiness or unhappiness, success or failure, contentment or discontentment, healthiness or unhealthiness, exultation or grief. All are natural states, and the list may go on and on. As with birth and illness, failure and grief are all natural. What could be more natural than to grieve over a child who has been handicapped and will suffer the consequences of that handicap throughout his life. A parent will not only grieve for his child, but will naturally grieve for himself and the trials that he must face due to the set of circumstances at hand.

In searching for methods of helping parents of the children that I have worked with, it became evident that the problem has often been acknowledged in our professional literature. It also became evident that very little has been written on how to help parents through the grieving process. Those books I found that dealt with the grieving process have typically been written by psychologists and the clergy and deal with death and dying.

Most authors speak of putting faith in God and taking one day at a time. They quote the Bible as saying, "Joy cometh in the morning." "They speak of coping with time, and again say," "God will help." "More useful, they say," "Concentrate on your loved one." "This approach may be helpful for those of deep religious faith. They may be able to turn to their church for emotional support. Often, however, the parents I have met are wondering how God could do this to their child and ask" "How could God let this happen?"

The prospect of a lifetime of pain and struggle may be overwhelming. The prospect of costly therapy to attain partial normalcy may cause the parents to cast about meaninglessly in search of answers that just are not there. We have seen the family that has spent numerous hours and dollars in search of someone who can change their child and his condition. We have also seen some professionals who refer the family on to other sources because they cannot help the family understand that the assistance at hand may be as good as they will find.

With these thoughts in mind I have set out to provide some tools that will assist parents through the grieving process. We are best prepared when we have information.

Ben Davidson, M.A.,CCC/SLP/IHS

Chapter 1

Many Kinds of Grief

Grief comes in many shapes and forms. It is unique, however, in that it requires honesty with others and with oneself. Regardless of the type of grief that a person suffers, he must take hold of it and handle it in a way that does not destroy him. Grief is real, and it is natural. It is a way of life. No one else will have the same set of circumstances or the same grief. A person and his grief are truly unique.

Parks, Collin, and Murray (19), in speaking of bereavement, state that a strong characteristic of grief is not prolonged depression, but acute episodic "pangs," a severe anxiety, and psychological pain. They continue by pointing out that grief may be strong, weak, prolonged, immediate, or delayed. They also point out numerous physical discomforts that are associated with grieving. Among them are headaches, digestive disturbances, aching limbs, insomnia, irritability, restlessness, moodiness, loss of appetite, increased appetite, muscle tension, fatigue, poor memory, difficulty concentrating, allergic reactions, trembling hands, heart palpitations, dizziness, and shortness of breath. Parents in our own study often related their physical problems to being "worn down"with taking care of their child.

Persons in grief have a whole jungle of emotions. Those emotions may be expressed poetically through talking or crying. Others are expressed through ritual. Wherever there is grief, there is a need for it to be expressed in some way.

Generally speaking, there are five types of grief, and our own study has verified that they are true for those grieving for handicapped children.

Anticipatory Grief is a type of grief that is usually associated with children with handicaps. It is a grief that occurs in a longer term and typically has no end in sight. Even when a child has a relatively mild handicapping condition, a parent may grieve over the possible implications of what their child must undergo to overcome the problem. I have seen parents of children with minor speech problems agonize over whether to subject their child to speech therapy or not. They were afraid that it might call attention to their child and embarrass them.

With a child that is handicapped, anticipatory grief takes on a whole new meaning. Parents deal not only with the child's possibilities of success but also the probabilities of failure. They go through the developmental milestones worrying about how their child will react when it comes time for school, little league, dating, college, marriage, career choices, and what will happen when the parents are gone. Anticipating problems in the future can be time-consuming and painful.

Sudden or Traumatic Grief is that type of grief brought on by a sudden accident. A child may be brain damaged or physically handicapped as the result of birth trauma, accident, or illness. These events may cause problems that are permanent in nature. This type of injury is devastating in that a normal life has been taken away and replaced by abnormality. Parent guilt feelings over possible prevention of these effects may cause an overpowering grief of its own and has no predictable end. It carries the unremitting stress of perpetual sorrow. Will therapy and time return the child to normal? The parent—for lack of good, solid, predictable results—sees time and money going, for what? They often ask, "Is there no end to this?"

No End Grief is very often associated with children who have disabilities. Parent grief is renewed at each developmental milestone, and each achievement is followed by another hurdle to be conquered. Parents, typically, see no end in sight until they or their child dies. Then, the question of who will take care of their child after they are gone adds a whole new dimension to their anxiety. Anger becomes one of the major characteristics involved in this type of grief. You weather one storm to meet the next one head-on.

Near-Miss Grief is that grief that exists because of what "might have been." "This grief is predominant when a normal person has suffered an accident that removes his normalcy. The grief of what might have been" "if." "If" becomes a big word in the near-miss grief business.

I remember a young man who had finished high school as an honor graduate and had received a full scholarship to a good university. During the summer before he was to enter the university, he had a stroke. His future was uncertain. His family grieved over what he could have been "if." His mother said that even though he had never made a grade less than a B, she could never remember a semester when she did not worry about whether he would pass or not. You can see what a problem this poor woman would face when she learned that her son might not be able to go to college. She had a real grief to work through.

With some good therapy and gutsy performance by the young man, he did, indeed, go back to college and got his degree in math. He became an excellent math teacher and was a super human being. He did, however, walk with a cane. His mother, many years later, still grieves over what might have been if he had not had his stroke.

As a therapist involved with this young man, I searched the literature for something to help this poor woman. I found nothing. That was when I decided to write this book.

Pathological Grief is grief that is closely related to near-miss grief. These people tend to hang on to the prospects of "what if" until they become pathologically ill themselves. They actually have a physical or mental illness as a result of their involvement with grief.

Gorer (5), in studies of "Death, Grief, and Mourning," in Britain, found that widows show a definite tendency to have more colds, flu, allergies, and mental depressions during the year following the loss of a loved one. This would not be unreasonable to expect in a person who is suffering grief due to being in possession of a handicapped child. It would, in fact, appear to be more likely as the expected term of grief is longer and the physical demands are greater. Indeed, we have frequently talked to parents who state that their own tendency to illness is probably the result of being "run-down" physically from the constant stress and fatigue of caring for their disabled child.

Generally speaking, grief takes on several predictable stages. Depending on the individuals involved, each stage of grief may vary in intensity and duration. Each individual may handle or discard a stage of grief in his own style. Each stage, however, will be addressed in some form during the grief process.

During the grief process, a person will find himself going through many emotions. These too are normal, and if the person does not feel these intense feelings then he is abnormal. Grief, frustration, anger, guilt, hostility, helplessness, depression, and loss of power are all normal emotions. It appears that they are just more intense when dealing with a handicapped child. This is probably due to the lack of information that the person has at hand.

Perhaps one of the most devastating feelings that will be encountered is the feeling of a "loss of power." It is not uncommon to see a man who has had it all and conquered it all break down and cry over his handicapped child. For once in his life, he does not know where, what, or how to fight. His bag of tricks and answers did not include these questions. He does not know what to do. He has handled all of the other emotions in his life, but in the past he has always had a hold on the problem and could find some ways around or over it. Now he is faced with something that may be completely foreign, and no one seems to have the answers. By the time we see these individuals, they may have been told what the problem is, or they may have been sent from doctor to therapist to teacher to center without finding out what will cure or help their child.

A large, brawny professional football player once sat in my office, holding his wife and crying for thirty minutes with relief. He had been to seven doctors and five centers for handicapped children before coming to us. What I had said to bring his tears of relief was this: "Your son has cerebral palsy. It is not curable, but we have an excellent program that will help him to achieve his maximum potential. You've brought him to the right place."

After the crying was over, he and his wife spent nearly an hour telling me about the tests that their child had been put through only to be referred to another doctor or center where the whole process began again. He had spent an enormous amount of money over a six-month period and still was not sure what it was that was wrong with his child. It happens much too often and is one of the blackest marks on the medical and paramedical professions.

We have too long stood aloof and performed our tests and asked our questions about family and medical history. Further grief, anxiety, and guilt are added to the family who has already felt these emotions because of the situation.

After over forty years of dealing with handicapped children and their parents, I find it little wonder that they go through stages of extreme depression. It is no surprise that they end up having bizarre thoughts and act a little strange at times. They struggle with the spiritual meaning of what is happening and search for the meaning of their lives as well as the answers to their child's problems.

Families fall apart as rage-despair-bitterness and hopelessness take over their lives. Parents need to take an active stand for the benefit of their child and themselves. They need to demand answers, even if the answer is "I don't know." You only get better with information, time, and care.

The following chapters of this book will address the previously mentioned conditions and how I, and other professionals, have helped parents and their children. The answer, contrary to some trends over the last years, is not to teach parents to be teachers of their own children. They have enough problems of their own in grieving, staying married, and staying well.

After interviewing over two hundred parents, I have found their grief is not unlike other forms of grief, but it appears to be much more intense because there is no end in sight. It is with them every minute of every day and will be as long as they and their child live.

Each of the following chapters will deal with some aspect of grief and how some families have handled it or how they were helped to handle it. If I can but remove one thorn from your pathway, the time and effort will have been well spent.

Chapter 2

Stages of Grief

The grief process has only been studied as a science over the last five decades. Most of the research that has been done has been in the areas of death and dying. Nearly all studies were done by psychiatrists, psychologists and clergy in an attempt to assist those who had lost a close member of their family or were themselves dying. In our own area of endeavor, we have found that social workers appear to be most familiar with the type of grief that parents of handicapped children go through. There have been several articles written by social workers on this subject. Parks (20), in her article in "Health and Social Work," clearly defines what parents are going through and laid out some tasks that help people through their grief. These tasks and thoughts will be discussed in the final chapter of this book. It has been noted, also, during our own studies that the grief process is much the same for a handicapped child's parents and that the same types of grief apply as in death and dying.

Generally speaking, a parent will go through all of the stages of grief. They may brush one aside or they may linger in another longer than expected. It has been observed, however, that if a person can be brought to an understanding with his grief, he will handle it in a routine way and will progress through the ordeal and come out the other end a whole person. Need I say that as a whole person he will be of much more benefit to himself, his family, and his handicapped child.

The stages of grief have been observed to take from three months to years, depending upon the variables. It has been recognized by myself and others working in this field that anything over two years is too long. It has also been observed that with assistance in understanding the grief process, it does not have to last this long to be effective in returning the person to normalcy.

Kavanaugh (8), in his book on "Facing Death," has listed seven stages of grief. Although other authors may use other terms, they in effect become synonymous in that nearly all authorities agree that the stages are fairly uniform, and each is unique. The seven stages listed by Kavanaugh are in complete agreement with what we found in our studies of families with handicapped children.

The first stage of grief that a parent might go through when they learn that their child has problems is shock. That is a feeling of disbelief when you first get the news. It is a time when denial is evident. Parents in our study reported that they just could not believe that it was true. "This just could not be happening to me," they said. "This is a mistake. They'll come back and tell me everything is OK." One parent I talked to said that she thought she was having a bad dream when she received the news that her child had serious problems. For weeks she expected to wake up and find that her child was alright.

Another parent said that she was fully convinced that the doctors and nurses did not know what they were talking about. Still another mother stated that she knew that the doctors were being honest, but she felt that her child would some day prove them wrong. This had never happened in her family or her husband's. "It was just their first impression," she said. "My child will come out of it." The denial process is often expressed by those having bad experiences. It is not uncommon for a bereaved spouse to expect his loved one to walk through the door even though he knows that person is dead. It is the same with parents who are wishing for the best for their child. We often hear the expression "He'll outgrow it." I find that this expression has been much overused by pediatricians when answering parents' anxious questions. I would suggest that we, as professionals, sometimes use the denial process ourselves. I cannot count the times I have continued therapy beyond all expectations because I was not willing to admit that a child was not capable of going further. Of course, I always justified it by saying, "I'd rather err in the child's benefit." Shortly after the shock wears off, a parent may enter the stage of disorganization. A numbness sets in while you try to rationalize and absorb the shock. This may be nature's way of providing a cushion for the pain while a person tries to find a rationale that will be acceptable to his way of thinking. It is perhaps the body's way of trying not to hurt so badly. Everything goes on hold while you try to make some sense out of the situation. At this stage a parent may not be able to talk about the problems. They may not be able to come up with appropriate questions or answers. In some cases parents say they are not able to consider other problems of normal living. Their total consciousness is directed toward the problems of their child, yet they are not able to think clearly about those problems or make any progress in handling the problems that are evident.

One father described his numbness this way. He said, "I have been successful in business and in my personal life because I understand business and people. Now, I am faced with this thing that I do not understand. I have no bag of tricks to rely on, and I am just stuck here. I can't go forward or backward." The next stage of grief is one of volatile emotions. It is a stage where mixed belief and disbelief begin to soak into the mind. The numbness wears off and then comes the pain. It is that period of mourning when a person can sob without control or shame. It is also a period that can be a mixture of two stages of grief, or it may be a transitional period. Some authors, such as Kubler-Ross (11), separate the two, but in dealing with parents of handicapped children we often see parents exhibiting symptoms of depression and hostility during these times of disbelief.

Parents often describe these periods as times when they recognize that their child has problems and they mourn over what is and what might have been. Then, at rational moments, they can't quite accept this drastic change in their life, and they become angry to the point that they want to lash out and hit someone. Professional people often become the target because parents feel frustration over the fact that the doctor and the therapists are not more helpful, or they might know something that they are not sharing with the parent. One parent put it rather pointedly when he said, "If you know what is wrong, say so. If you do not know what is wrong, say so. Is that asking too much?" As a professional person who has spent many years working with handicapped children, I have tried to become more human when dealing with parents. I know that many professional people struggle with this problem. They don't want to become too familiar with family members. Perhaps, if we shared with parents our own feelings as we fight the battle for their child, they would understand that parents, doctors, teachers, and therapists are just people, doing the best they can under difficult circumstances. I hope that parents can understand we also grieve for your child.

At one time in my career, I was director of a pilot project doing work and research on what we could do to help severe or multiply handicapped infants. The babies were from three years of age and younger. On one occasion, when I was giving a mother her baby and a quick report before I started the next session, I quickly turned and headed off down the hall. The mother commented to our nurse, "That was abrupt." The nurse replied, "He didn't want you to see him cry." That mother chased me down the hall and gave me a big hug.

Another emotion that rears its ugly head during this stage of grief is guilt. As parents' emotions run the gamut, they often begin to wonder how they contributed to their child's problems. Was it genes or not eating right? Did that fall in the yard cause brain damage? Did smoking, drugs, or alcohol cause it? Did the mother miss taking her prenatal vitamins one day? These are the basic questions. When a parent's mind goes to work on it, some of the guilt feelings are far out, unreal, and irrational.

When a parent gets through the guilt stage and the depression that goes with it, he may enter a period of loss and loneliness. This is a time of feeling sorry for one's self and his child. You begin to realize that this is reality and that you are going to have to live with it for the rest of your natural life. When this reality sets in, many parents experience periods of relief. They express it by saying, "I've made it this far. Maybe we'll be OK." During this period, you might get along quite well for a period of time, and then it hits again. Maybe you see another handicapped child or even a normal child who appears to be what you were expecting. Maybe it is a time when your child reaches a landmark and does not perform as well as other children his age. It is a regression.

Most parents agree that the periods of regression become fewer and farther between, thus making the periods of relief more meaningful. It is at these times parents start making decisions about what to do now. It is in this stage of reestablishment that important decisions are made. Without help, some parents make the wrong decisions and further ruin their future hopes for happiness.

During the reestablishment stage, many mothers decide to make it up by devoting the rest of their life to the handicapped child. Some even go so far as to take in all handicapped children. They enter parent groups, volunteer groups, advocacy groups, and so on. There is no end to their desire to do good. This is good if it does not get out of control. Often, in these cases, the mother becomes mentally separated from the rest of the family. On the other hand, with the huge medical and rehabilitation bills, it is not uncommon to see a father devote himself completely to making a living, nothing else. All of this may seem perfectly logical to the distressed mind.

This final stage of grief, if handled properly, may be the most important thing that happens to a handicapped child. If the family can adjust, reestablish, and go on as a family, then the family members will support each other and grow. If the family splinters in their effort to handle their problems, then disaster is right around the corner.

These stages of grief may last for weeks, months, or even years. It has been shown time after time in our own studies that with some help and understanding parents can move through these stages in an orderly manner and maintain some semblance of life while doing so. In the end, if they come out a whole person and a whole family, the handicapped child will receive more advantage and assistance.

Chapter 3

Grief as Helplessness

Grief includes helplessness, a feeling of being lost and out of control. Helplessness is closely related to loss of power but may be a more severe and complicated emotion to deal with. It is more like they are berating themselves for having lost control and not knowing how to deal with it. Many parents express their helplessness, and even if they are not able to openly admit that they are not in control, they will often envy those who seem to have everything going the way they want it. They often berate themselves because they are not able to take hold of their problems and go on with their life. It is expressed in many ways by different people.

A police officer said, "Give me a maniac with a gun pointed at my head, and I know what to do. Give me a pregnant woman having a baby in the back of a car, and I can handle it. Give me a domestic quarrel between two hostile adults, and I can work something out. Put my son in my arms, and I am completely helpless." Helplessness is a new emotion for this and other parents of handicapped children. It is something that they feel that they just can't handle. Maybe, until this time, they have felt some minimal amount of control. Now they have something that they can't control.

Helplessness is one of the most frequently stated problems of those in the grief process. It may be the strongest emotion that they feel. It inhibits their responses to the other stages of grief that they go through. In most instances, it accompanies all other emotions that are expressed. It is like something has taken over their lives, and it controls them even when they don't want it to. The lack of knowledge, the anger, the sorrow, tearing of eyes, the urge to "cry out" or to "strike out" is almost uncontrollable at times.

One young mother who was street-bred, born tough, said that she was raised not to get mad, just to get even. "How do you get even with a helpless, handicapped baby?" she asked.

The depression that comes with these feelings of helplessness can best be treated if it is expected. Some people who "held up" during the periods of crisis and actually carried the load and family on their shoulders are surprised years later to find that the depression that everyone else felt and worked through has finally caught up with them. If the whole family is aware of the situation, then this delayed depression can also be treated. It is not uncommon, however, to see a family fall apart years later because no one understands that the mother or father never had their chance to be depressed or to express their hurt and anger. Even though this pattern can work both ways, it is most common to see the father, who took the lead in "being strong" because it was expected of him, fall apart at a much later date. He just never had his chance to grieve. It is notable that depression keeps coming up in nearly every stage and type of grief.

Many men have been taught all of their life not to show emotion. It is not considered manly in our society for a man to cry or lash out at those around him in his frustration and anger.

I'll never forget the middle-aged lawyer who appeared to have everything under control. He went about his business of taking care of his handicapped daughter's needs with business-like precision. During her first two years of treatment, his wife and I went through many tearful sessions because he did not seem to sympathize or share her feelings. Then, one day, right in the middle of a progress report conference, he called me an "arrogant son of a bitch." His outburst came without provocation and thoroughly shocked his wife. When he got through reaming me out, he quickly got his composure back and began to apologize. I told him, "Don't stop now. That's the most meaningful thing you've said in two years." During that session, we found out that he did care. He was terribly upset, and he and his wife had a lot in common in the way of helpless feelings. Needless to say, they made some good gains after that in becoming a family unit again. I made some points with them and the social worker involved for keeping my cool and not taking it personally.

During these times of helplessness, it is not uncommon to see a family divide into two camps. Men often justify giving their attention to the other children by saying, "After all, she is tied up with the new baby 24/7." Dad feels an obligation to make it up to the other children for the loss of their mother. At the same time, Mom feels the isolation from the rest of the family and in turn tries to make up to the new baby for the loss of his father, brothers, and sisters. It is a vicious circle that grows and becomes harder and harder to break.

The "helpless" syndrome is best solved by team effort. If a family can be made to understand what is happening and share those feelings with each other, then they are not so alone. They can take corrective measures to overcome those feelings. Often a simple explanation can redirect their thinking. At other times, it is a long difficult process that requires extensive counseling.

Many teachers and therapists are not equipped to handle this type of counseling. I was fortunate to have received training in counseling and have been able to help some families through this process. If a therapist or teacher is not able to handle counseling tasks, then he can become invaluable to a psychologist or social worker in pointing out the stages of grief that the family appears to be going though and how it appears to be handling it. It gives the counselor a starting point and an understanding of what the family is going through. In cases that have needed counseling in greater depth than I have been able to give, counselors have given very positive feedback to the information that has been provided for them. In some instances, I have been invited to attend some sessions with the parents, and it has been to my benefit to have attended.

The helplessness suffered in grief is a very real and critical issue. It is, perhaps, one of the most difficult problems to overcome.

Chapter 4

Grief and Depression

Depression is a natural part of grief and may come long after the incident that caused that grief. As you will notice, depression is frequently associated with other kinds and stages of grief. It may appear with each and every stage, or it may be years later before a person suffers the crying spells, loss of appetite, feeling "down," or avoidance of relationships with those around him. Over half of all marriages involving handicapped children break up. Many of them break up years later when the child is out of the home. Indications are that many parents are so involved in caring for the child, the family, etc., that they do not have a chance to grieve.

Adult family members such as grandparents may also be involved in a grief process of their own. This may isolate them from the family at a time they are really needed for support. As one grandmother put it, "It just hurt too bad, seeing my child and grandchild both suffering, I just couldn't be strong enough to be there." Fleishman (3), in his article on low birth weight infants, points out the depression that parents go through. He talks about how mothers feel an acute sense of failure. Fathers focus on the monumental costs of care and the future costs of rehabilitation and education. He also indicates that fathers typically focus on the child's weakness rather than his strength. Parents are depressed over the loss of the expected perfect child and begin to go through the grief process during these times. Fleishman also makes the point that grandparents may also go through these same feelings of anger, denial, and depression. He points out that negative feelings such as revulsion at the abnormal, inadequacy of reproduction, inadequacy of rearing, anger, shock, guilt, and embarrassment also create and add to more depression.

In our own study, we found similar conditions and added that stress, anxiety, and higher levels of psychiatric symptoms are more likely to meet the criteria for depressive disorders. We find that mothers of handicapped children typically show less enjoyment of the child and a tendency toward isolation. Along with everything else, they have a negative image of themselves. Many dwell on the thought of, "What will others think of us now?" In their studies of families with handicapped children, Veisson, Shar, and Magi (22) studied and compared families with normal children and families with handicapped children. Among their findings, they concluded that mothers of children with Down's syndrome and mothers of children with motor handicaps suffered less depression. There were no conclusions as to why. It just got reported that way.

In our lives we play many roles. We might be wife, husband, child, parent, bill payer, gardener, organizer, mess maker, student, teacher, cook, compliment giver, criticizer, and confidante. The list goes on and on. When a handicapped child enters the picture, many roles change instantly. Some roles are eliminated, and some are added, wanted or not. Some roles may be left unfulfilled.

Consider the father. What role will he play now that a child is here? He will continue to be the provider of the living. He will continue to support his wife. He will now have the added responsibility of the child. What else can we expect from him? Perhaps we can expect grief, mourning, and depression. He will not only be considering those things mentioned before such as additional costs, but also he will have the expected grief process for his child, the grief for what this has done to his wife, plus the grief that has been added to his own life. That is three grief processes at one time in a society that tells him, "Suck it up and do your job." Consider the other children in the family. Will they be embarrassed to let their friends see their handicapped brother or sister? Probably. Will they be socially isolated from their friends because they can't bring them into their home anymore? Probably. Will they grieve for the life that their new brother or sister will have to live because of the handicapping conditions? Probably. Will they grieve for what Mom and Dad are going through? Probably. Will they get a chance to express that grief and go on with their life as they were doing? Probably not. Children suffer too in these trying times. It is often what makes fathers turn to them and try to make up the difference.

Another depressing thought that so many parents go through is, "What will the rest of the family think? How will they accept us now?" You cannot predict how grandparents, aunts, uncles, nephews, nieces, and cousins will respond. In the best of situations, they will be supportive and helpful. In the worse-case scenario, they will withdraw and isolate the family. Many parents go through a period of doubt and think, "How will we break it to the family?" Webster's II New College Dictionary defines "depression" as a neurotic or psychotic condition marked by an inability to concentrate, insomnia, and feelings of dejection and guilt. That pretty well defines what parents of handicapped children go through. Yet, it is much more complicated than that. If they could go through one grief process and be done with it, then everything would be alright. Instead, parents must go through a series of depressions related to their feelings of loss (for the child they did not get), for the suffering of their child (what he must go through in this lifetime), for personal loss (how their lifestyle has changed), for other family members (how their lives have been effected), and for what is to come (how each landmark in their child's life will be effected).

Parents in our study have described their feelings quite well. They state that they go through a period of withdrawal from life. They feel as if they are in a fog, intensely sad, and often wondering if there is any reason to go on. They complain that their lives appear to be completely pointless at this stage of their life. Such questions arise as, "Why get up? Why bother to eat? Why even stop eating? Why bathe? Why get dressed? Why even bother to be depressed?" I will state again, "To not be depressed would be very abnormal." Clinical depression, if left untreated, would lead to a worsening of a person's mental state. But in grief that is due to a good reason, depression is a way for nature to protect us by shutting down the nervous system so that we can adapt to the new situation that we feel that we can't handle. If the grief process is healing, then depression is one of the many steps that we must take along that path to recovery.

Kubler-Ross and Kessler (15), in their book "On Grief and Grieving," state that "seeking a way out of depression feels like going into a hurricane and sailing around the inside perimeter, fearful that there is no exit door." They also conclude, "When you allow yourself to experience depression, it will leave as soon as it has served its purpose in your loss." Our present-day society appears to be in a "stamp out depression" mode. In the event of clinical depression, some intervention may be needed. But, when depression serves its purpose and moves on, it is good. Unfortunately, we have television ads that offer drugs for normal, natural depression. We are a society of "quick fix." The use of drugs to assist with depression is referred to by some as a "balancing act." We need to accept some depression in our lives as normal, yet be willing to treat the abnormal. How do we determine the difference? If it doesn't go away after a couple of months, it might be time to seek a professional opinion. In severe cases, professional counseling and appropriate medications may be called for. This should only be as a last resort. Don't let anyone tell you that you should not be sad.

For all of the reasons a person may be depressed, we tend to forget the preparatory grief that a person has to undergo in order to prepare himself for what is to come. It is not a grief of loss but of impending loss. One of the thoughts that parents carry and are depressed about is the future of their child. With most children, we look forward to the day that they grow up, become independent, and leave the "nest." It depresses most parents of handicapped children to think, "What will happen to my child when I die? Who will take care of him?" It is a legitimate concern. Fortunately, in these later times, the state and federal governments have invested heavily in schools and halfway houses that provide for handicapped individuals who reach adulthood.

Parents should not look at the "sunny side" at times like this, even if they can find one. It is a time to grieve and understand what is happening and what is going to happen. You as a parent are losing so much yet gaining in another way. It is a time to grieve, accept reality, survive, and go forward.

This chapter is short, but it was meant to only define and illustrate the depression suffered by parents and families. Depression will rear its ugly head throughout the remainder of the book in association with other thoughts and concerns.

Chapter 5

Bizarre Thoughts and Actions

Grief is not a mental illness. The insanity of grief, however, is that the rest of the world seems to go on oblivious of a person's pain. Parents often wonder if anyone in the whole world understands or knows of their situation and their grief. "Does anybody care?" they ask. Some people, by nature, understand the personal aspect of grief and accept the shortcomings of others during their grief process.

Some people become psychotic over their bereavement as a precipitating, not a causal factor. They may demonstrate bizarre, hard-to-imagine thoughts and behaviors. These people may lose touch with reality and retreat into their own mental world of horror and as often as not contemplate death as the only possible end to their agony. Some retreat beyond that point and find themselves unable to even organize a thought as meaningful as that. It is at such times that the persons come under the care of a psychiatrist and receive the psychological and medical treatment that is necessary to help them.

When a person has reached a state of psychosis, he usually drops out of sight. The psychiatrist takes over the complicated treatment, and we, as professionals and paraprofessionals, are left out. If things go well, we are left treating the child while his mother or father receives needed treatment. In searching for ways to help parents of the children that I have worked with, I have found that there is very little meaningful literature on the subject.

Because we are not involved in psychiatric care, again, this chapter may be short. We are not going to try to intercede at this level. It is critical, however, that we understand something of what happens, and it is imperative that we recognize the symptoms so that we might make proper referrals when we see, you, the parent, cross that line.

When thoughts and behaviors become too bizarre, psychiatric treatment is a must, especially if the psychosis inhibits the person's ability to function. We have at times been alerted by the other parent when a person appears to be "out of touch." This is not a transitory and brief state of mind that the parent will progress through and come out whole. The sooner the treatment is provided, the better the results will be.

In our experiences, we have seen parents who became incapable of providing the daily care needed by their handicapped child. One such case was a young mother who had lost one child in a house fire. The second child was left blind and badly scarred. The child's deformities as a result of the burns were horrible to look at. How should the mother of this child react when she, herself, was a nineteen-year-old child? Needless to say, she had severe problems that required intervention.

The father of the child was a salesman who was lucky to get home three weekends per month. This left the mother as the sole caregiver of this severely handicapped child.

The mother presented a cheerful appearance and acted as though everything was well in hand. She talked a good show, but when the child developed infections and other complications, an investigation revealed that the mother left the child unattended for long periods of time. The daily baths and dressings prescribed were actually being carried out once or twice per week. Through it all, the mother assured everyone that she could handle it, and everything was just fine. To all appearances, she was devoting her life to taking care of her child.

Under the care of a psychiatrist, it was discovered that the mother had made several unsuccessful attempts to end her own life and her child's. She prowled the bars at night, leaving the child alone at home at the age of two. She presented herself as single and at times spent the night away from home with men that she picked up at bars. At these times, she literally removed the child from her consciousness and believed the role that she was playing. Through psychological counseling and medication, she was eventually returned to a functional person who faced the reality of the situation and assumed proper care for her child.

Under psychosis, we have seen parents who believed that their child's problems would go away. They felt that the child would outgrow the problem and that there was no need for concern. Other parents, while telling us that their child was handicapped, still had a vivid memory of what might have been. Others deny that there is a problem and act as though the professionals and others in their lives are going about some diabolical scheme to ruin their child's life.

We had a mother of a severely cerebral palsied, mentally retarded child assure us that her child could work math problems and write. She just didn't understand how we could report this boy's abilities as severely limited. She was so convinced that the child would not perform for us because we were not fair that she agreed to take the child into an observation room and elicit those academic behaviors for us. As we eagerly watched through a one-way mirror, the mother took a pencil, placed it in the boy's hand, gripped around his hand and guided him through working the math problems and writing his name. While she was assisting with these skills, the boy was looking over his left shoulder and drooling. The mother later triumphantly challenged us to prove that the child did not understand every problem and initiate the writing of his name. Fortunately, this mother did receive help and came to recognize the limitations of her son.

We have seen parents who feel that their child's handicapping conditions are a punishment administered by an angry God. They reason that the child is innocent, so the sin must be their own, and this is the way God is punishing them for their transgressions. Some go way back into their childhood to find sins that warrant this type of punishment. We have seen one or two instances where a parent says that "this is God's will and we won't interfere with that." In other words, don't try to help the child and change what God has done.

Wolfelt (24), in his book "Healing Your Grieving Heart," gives illustrations of people's thoughts and how they react to the old myths. He acknowledges that many people probably internalize many of our society's harmful myths about grief and mourning. He makes a good point by saying that some myths need to be let go. Some people say, "Be strong and carry on. Tears are a sign of weakness. I need to get over my grief. And this is something we don't talk about." He points out that these myths will cause you to feel guilty or ashamed of your true thoughts and feelings. He goes on to say, "Your grief is your grief. It's normal and necessary. Allow it to be what it is." To fight grief is to invite trouble. He goes on to discuss how sometimes mourners fall back on self-destructive behaviors to get through the difficult times. He recommends that you be honest with yourself about drug or alcohol abuse. If you are in over your head, ask for help. Are you having suicidal thoughts or feelings? Are you isolating yourself too much? Talk to someone today. Getting help is a form of compassionate self-care.

There are many reasons that people seek professional help, and we could spend a great deal of time listing symptoms and giving illustrations. Instead, let me just say that sometimes when a person is going through serious inner struggles, there are no friends available to listen to them. Even if friends are available, some people withdraw rather than burden their friends. At other times, a person might have enough insight to know that counseling will help him move through the healing process more rapidly. Others get psychiatric help because of recommendations made by other professionals with whom they come in contact.

Great tragedies are more likely to require psychotherapy because destruction is high after an earthquake. The parents or our patients are not the ones who have insecurities, anxieties, or personal problems they want to work out. These parents are the ones with specific, serious problems that they need to handle so that they may get back to the business at hand. Family members, teachers, therapists, doctors, and counselors should always be on the lookout for unusual behaviors or unusual thoughts that may be demonstrated by other family members of a handicapped child. It is always wise to look at the whole family. Parents, grandparents, and siblings are sometimes put under severe pressure when a handicapped child comes along. Parents should think in terms of treating the whole family for grief, not just the mother. Such treatment will be of benefit to each family member, including the handicapped child. Those handicapped persons who have achieved great things in their life nearly always give their family credit for making their lives possible.

Chapter 6

Intensification of Physical Illness

Intensification of physical illness is very common with families of handicapped children. It is natural for a worrying person not to get enough sleep. It is also natural for that person to neglect himself as he dedicates more and more of his time to thinking about and caring for the handicapped child. Physical health can break down under mental stress. In books on death and dying, many authors speak of this problem and how it affects the whole family. A mentally and physically exhausted body is subject to illness. We have seen it many times.

It was noted by Parkes, Colin, and Murray (19) that, generally, young people show more symptoms than older people. This has been our observation also and has caused us to talk with parents about all of their children, not just the handicapped one. We must remember that young people have very little experience with handling stress, and a severely handicapping condition of a child ranks very high in society's stressful situations.

Headaches are one of the most reported manifestations of stress that parents report. They relate their headaches to stress, loss of sleep, and fatigue. In most cases, they do not feel that it is a case for counseling or psychotherapy. They just want the doctor to give them some medication to rid themselves of this headache. They often turn to over-the-counter remedies. That is one of the difficult problems to handle in that our

34

society has become too fast moving. We want immediate cures for all of our problems. If you can take a pill and it goes away, why not?

Another symptom that constantly presents itself to parents of a handicapped child is that of digestive disturbances. Some of the parents in our study developed ulcers as a result of these continuing problems. We tend to see digestive problems particularly in parents who are harboring bitterness over their "lot in life." Their negative thoughts about themselves, their family situation, and what the future holds adds too much stress to their bodies if they don't find a way to grieve and get it out.

Some of the less specific problems that may occur as a result of grief are aching limbs, insomnia, irritability, restlessness, and moodiness. Most parents do not associate these aches and pains with their concern for their child. They usually just attribute these symptoms to just being exhausted from the physical pace that they must now keep. We had one mother who continually complained about the fatigue factor, the pace she must keep, and the overall exertion of dealing with her child. In reality, the grandmother took care of the new baby while the mom sat in her chair hour after hour grieving. It is usually the case that the symptoms persist even at times when the person is rested and the pace has slowed down for one reason or another. It is not uncommon to see family members lose weight or, in some cases, gain weight as they let themselves go under the weight of stress.

Of a more physical nature, many parents report that they have either a loss of appetite or increase of appetite due to their situation. Those parents who have a tendency to be overeaters anyway state that they have lost control. Perhaps one of the critical factors here is that the parent may have lost self-esteem as a result of having a handicapped child. They may feel that they have failed in the basic function of procreation. Moms are often plagued with questions like "What did I do wrong?" With the problems at hand, being neat and trim may not be a major priority. It is not unusual to hear the father complain about the wife's letting herself go and not caring about her appearance. Fathers in neat business suits and ragged, unkempt mothers become a common sight.

Muscle tension and fatigue also become common complaints as time marches on. Again, parents blame it on the time and energy consumed by caring for the handicapped child. In actuality, if a time schedule were kept, we would find that the parent may be doing no more now than they did before the child arrived. They are now involved in different activities that carry more mental stress than those previously practiced. It has been necessary, in our experience, to have some parents document their activities before and after the child was born. Only then could we talk to them logically about the prospect of their grieving process causing some of the problems that they were experiencing. Indeed, as is often the case, once a parent handles his grief process, he can go on to do more and be more physically active without the mentioned problems returning.

Another problem soon becomes evident. Many parents complain that they are undergoing one respiratory distress after another. Gorer (5), Kavanaugh (8), and Kubler-Ross (14) have all discussed the tendency of people under stress to have more allergic and respiratory problems. They were, of course, talking about cases involving death and dying. Our study has demonstrated that the same phenomenon takes place with those grieving for their handicapped child. In our case, however, the grief process does not include an ending. It is a never-ending thing that goes on until one or the other party dies.

"Fatigue" is the common word heard around parent groups. Many parents use it as a synonymous word for "exhausted." The hustle and bustle of life with a handicapped child doesn't leave a person "tired." "Fatigued" or "exhausted" are more descriptive and meaningful to these parents. You seldom just hear the word "tired" when talking to these people. Perhaps these words carry a meaning of more intensity than just plain tired. Those who have discussed it usually conclude that they do not wish to sound as if they are complaining. So, instead of going into how really, really, tired they are, they just use fatigued or exhausted to describe their condition. That lets other people draw their own conclusions.

In an attempt to get more definition in the terms that were being used by the parents in our parent groups, we asked them to define several terms. Included in those terms were the words "tired," "fatigued," and "exhausted." In nearly all instances, "tired" was described as a good feeling that resulted after strong physical activity, such as playing golf, swimming, running, or even doing house work or a job. "Fatigued" elicited such responses as being mentally and physically exhausted, leaving the person with a feeling of remorse or bitterness. The term "exhausted" was the ultimate "tired." When the parents were "exhausted," it was a way of saying, "Leave me alone. I have had it. I can't take any more."

Some parents reported that they suffered from poor memory and extreme difficulty in concentrating. The handicapped child and his needs seem to crowd out all other thoughts. Things often do not get done because they are just plain forgotten. When the person attempts to read and understand something, he finds himself rereading and studying information, trying to figure out what it means. This quality should remind parents to ask for repeats or get it in writing when professionals are giving them reports about their child. At least, with a written copy, they can go over it later and try to absorb the content of what was said. We should also remember that this information was written by professionals who have their own jargon that they toss around. They use meaningless initials that they are familiar with. If a parent does not call them to a halt and ask for an explanation, the information goes right over their heads. I have never seen a professional person who did not appreciate the fact that a person asked for clarity of what was being said.

When written information is passed out to parents, it is often done with the idea of giving that parent some good data that they can use. Again, most of it was written by professionals who still have that tendency to use language that is not understood by everyone. As a parent, it is your responsibility to call them on it. Go back and explain that it does not make sense or that you do not understand the terminology. They will explain. Insist on it.

In group sessions, I found parents were hesitant to admit their ignorance of the terms being used or the language content. In many cases, I came to realize that they did not know enough to ask a good question. They were just waiting for someone to fill them in with enough information that they could ask a decent question. In some cases, we found that, in their confused state, the parent thought he understood the material but in reality did not. That is one reason to ask for a list of terms with definitions to be provided at all group sessions and discussed. It would clarify a great deal, and parents would then know more about what was going on.

Do not hesitate to talk to the professionals in your life about your concerns. I will never forget the little, teenage mom who stopped the speaker at a parent group and asked, "When do we get to discuss our problems?" In many cases, parent groups turn in to lecture sessions where knowledgeable people give informative speeches. There is definitely room for that. But, to get to the heart of what parents need to know, let them speak. Parents, you need to insist on it.

You would be amazed at some of the definitions that parents will give for such terms as retarded, brain damaged, cerebral palsied, hypertension, and hypotension. The list goes on and on. The words that get bantered around so much that they become common are often new and frightening to a parent with a handicapped child. Parents should always demand clarification of terms used. I found it refreshing when a parent said, "Wait a minute. What the heck does that mean?" In nearly every case, other parents in the group nodded their approval.

We have found in our studies that parents of handicapped children also suffer a worsening of allergic reactions. We have found other studies that confirm our data. Parents of handicapped children suffer more of worsening allergic reactions. People under stress have twice as many respiratory infections as those who are not. This can be expected in light of the previously mentioned problems. If a person runs himself down physically, mentally, and every other way, allergies come to the front. If the person is suffering from poor memory, as mentioned before, he may have forgotten to take allergy medication or to clean the dust from the house in their usual routine. It is common oversights that add to these problems of people in grief.

Some parents talk of their nerves being "shot." They report that they are a "nervous wreck" and that their hands actually tremble. Some report heart palpitations and other signs of nervous disorders. Heart palpitations, dizziness, and shortness of breath become commonplace in this population. These are all signs of a "nervous breakdown" in some parent's way of thinking. They become frightened that they will become incapacitated from their nervous condition. This just adds stress to the overload of stress that they are already experiencing.

We should recognize that the symptoms mentioned in this chapter are common, everyday phenomena that occur in all people's lives. It is just that they are intensified when stress is mounted upon stress with no end in sight. Add to all of this stress and confusion the fact that you do not know how or why this handicapped child has happened, and you have the perfect program for disaster.

Chapter 7

A Spiritual Struggle and Search for Meaning

At the time of catastrophe, nearly all persons will question a God who allows such tragedy into their lives. A handicapped child is such a tragedy. Even a non-Christian may trouble his soul with the big "Why?" The struggle with powerlessness can be a religious or a non-religious experience. The question, "Why me, Lord?" has been asked many times over far less significant problems than that of a handicapped child. It is at such times that some people lose their faith in God and in their church. There are numerous stories of people who have withdrawn from all religious activity in their time of stress. On the other hand, there are those who lean heavily on their religious beliefs to see them through a mountain of problems.

At such times, it is normal for parents to wonder how others can go on with their lives as if nothing has happened. As one parent asked, "My world has come to an end. Doesn't anyone care?" Pastor Rusty Davidson (2), in his book "In The Hands of God," quotes Lamentations 1:12, "Is it nothing to you all who pass by?" God has made sacrifices for us. How can we question his need for us to make some sacrifices? One parent said, "Why not me? This baby needs me." Some religious people have their faith sorely tried by their belief that God can accomplish miracles. They pray for this burden to be lifted from their child. They ask God to provide the funds needed to pay for the expensive care needed. They know in their heart that God could fix everything, if he just would. At these times, parents are on the edge of losing faith and trying to handle the problems on their own. It is a poor trade and is nearly always disastrous.

There are some religious beliefs that prohibit a person from allowing treatment of their child. In such cases, religious freedom, as guaranteed by the first amendment of our constitution, ensures that person's right to refuse treatment because this problem is "God's will." There have been court cases where others have tried to step in and assume the parents' rights and responsibility. In nearly all such cases, they have lost unless there was a life-threatening situation. It is not our purpose, here, to pursue the right and wrong of such measures. It is more our purpose to inform you, the reader, that these possibilities are present and you may, as a parent, be forced to deal with them. The action you take must be your own. No one can make those decisions for you. I have, myself, been faced with a parent who said, "We can't go against God's will." Davidson (2) speaks of how we love our children. Indeed, he points out how we love them from the first moment following their birth. He goes on to say, "To understand God's love, you have to understand God. This is no easy task. It is worth noting, however, that there is no scripture in the Bible that says God will spare us the trials of this life. It is a given that we will have troubles and trials accompanied by pain and grief. That's life. Thus, the question, "Why not me?" Davidson (2) also quotes Psalm 18:35. "You give me your shield of victory, and your right hand sustains me; you stoop down to make me great." He goes on to say, "We have a God who loves us so much and desires only the best for us." Verse 20 chapter 17 of Matthew ends by saying, "And nothing shall be impossible unto you." So, keep to your faith and give it a chance.

Parents are entitled to freedom of worship. Their right to believe as they will is undeniable. There are those who believe, however, that this applies only as long as their beliefs don't give them a license to violate the rights of others. Only by closing their eyes to the injustices that they are doing to their handicapped child can some parents find peace of mind in their faith.

The Reverend John D. Lee, in a little booklet titled "Why Did This Have To Happen To Me?" suggests a different faith when he wrote:

"A Christian looks at suffering in this manner: 'Here,' he says to himself, 'is a condition. It is present. It is real. Since it exists, then God has permitted it to exist. And, since God has permitted it, he has a purpose in it. My task is to find out, if I can, what purpose God has in mind for me, what final goal he hopes to bring about. Obviously, what he wants me to become is still possible for me with this pain and this suffering. What does God want me to do with it, so that, through it I can become the kind of person God wants me to become?' To do this, take pain and suffering and put it in its proper place. No longer can one sit and bemoan one's lot, as though it were much, much worse than that of anyone else. One must, to bring one's grief out into the open, look at it steadily and then, with the best that we can understand of what God wants us to do with it, proceed to that end.

Reverend Lee suggests that the question "Why did this have to happen to me?" is quite presumptuous. "Well, why not?" he asks. "Are we fate's favorites, out of all mankind?" Suffering is a common lot. Literally no one gets through this life without a certain amount of suffering.

In the preceding paragraphs, there is an obvious conclusion that problems can and do exist. They are a reality of life. They must be faced squarely and learned to be managed so that they do not destroy us and those around us. We can never be happy without the management of problems.

Dr. Robert Youngs (26), in an article written for the Laymen's Movement for a Christian World, said:

"The Bible reminds us that good people sometimes suffer because God, through nature, can be no respecter of persons. (He maketh his sun to rise on the evil and on the good, and sendeth rain on the just and on the unjust.) This is a world of law and order, where all people are subject to cause and effect regardless of their virtue or lack of it. Good people are just as susceptible as bad people when they are exposed to contagious diseases. They strike the ground just as forcibly when they slip and fall. The world would be an unscientific and unpredictable place in which to live if it were not this way." The point to be made to parents who are feeling injustice is that certain laws govern natural phenomena and produce order in our world. God works in lawful and orderly ways. This world is organized in a wonderful way. It contains good and bad. The belief that, in our time, God works through men has provided spiritual strength to many parents. God's miracle today may be the doctor's and therapist's use of the intelligence and skill that God has given them. It has been said, "That woman was an absolute angel." I have heard it more than once. My question is, "How do we not know that the spirit of an angel might enter the body of a human being and cause that person to do what was needed at the right time?" I believe in the spirit of God, the spirit of man, and the spirit of angels.

A few short years ago, I was very ill. I had an infection that got into my bloodstream. At the time I felt bad, but it wasn't critical enough to cause me concern. I believe God intervened at just the right time. As I came home that day, I noticed that there were not any cars at the health clinic. So, I just stopped by to head off a serious illness. If the clinic had been busy, I would not have stopped. In short order, the doctor had me flat on my back in the hospital with an IV of Cipro flowing into my veins. For thirteen days, I was in that position.

While I was hospitalized, I went down fast and reached the point of having hallucinations. I noticed that there were three people in the room that I did not know and appeared to be unacknowledged by nurses, family, and friends who came by. They stood by my bed, waiting. On occasion, one would hold out his hand to me, and on occasion I reached to take it. But, I always drew back, knowing that if I took hold, I would be gone. On the day that the doctor said that my white blood cell count was on its way back down, they left. I am convinced that those three beings were angels. Some might say it was just a hallucination. Maybe, who knows?

Kubler-Ross and Kessler (15), in their book on "Grief and Grieving," have included a section on angels. They report that, many times, dying people see angels. On one instance a woman reported to her husband and the hospital chaplain that she had seen angels. When the chaplain, later, reported her acknowledgement to her doctor, the doctor said, "That's never a good sign." He had been there before and knew what was coming. From my own experience, I have to agree with her statement, "They were beautiful." When the doctor said, "That's never a good sign," the chaplain said, "Not medically, but spiritually, it's perfect." Kubler-Ross and Kessler (15), in the same section, speak of some people having strong beliefs in angels and guardian angels, while others hope they exist. We speak of them in many forms in our culture: the angel of death, angels we pray to for help and comfort. Many times we just ask for help. As I look back at my own life, I feel that I positively have a guardian angel who has protected me in some dangerous situations. As I worked with handicapped children, I often felt a guiding hand. Either that or I just had a bunch of kids who really made me look good.

Many people believe that you cannot die alone. There are always angels there to be with you. Young children often refer to angels as their playmates. Infants often look into the corner of a room, smile, and vocalize as if they were talking to someone. They have been called everything from "guides" to "spooks." I believe that you cannot die alone and you cannot grieve alone. They will be with you whether you recognize them or not. Grieving people have said, "In my darkest days, I was carried by angels." I say from the bottom of my heart, "On the long road you now walk alone, you have unseen companions." We all have angelic moments that we give each other. They appear as simple acts of kindness. Kubler-Ross and Kessler (15) say, "It may not seem to matter much, but they save lives by lifting others from sadness. While angels watch us, we are capable of being each other's angels." In deep grief, a person may ask, "Where are my angels?" while they miss all of the angelic people around them. Are angels using real people to accomplish their mission? I wouldn't be surprised.

Faith in religion is such a highly personal thing that it is very difficult, if not impossible, to actually know how others believe and how their beliefs affect their peace of mind. Is a parent so dependent on God's will that he won't carry out therapy at home? Will he feel that it makes no difference because "God's will be done" ? Or, on the other hand, will he believe that God is working through man and carry out every instruction tediously that has been recommended by the doctor or therapist?

A prayer used by alcoholics at the AA meeting is also applicable here: "God, give us the ability to change what can be changed, the strength to accept what cannot be changed, and the wisdom to know the difference." Parents who know that they have done their best and that their child has achieved all that he can possibly achieve will at last find peace of mind. That is not to say that the problem will go away. Where there is healing, there are scars. But, to my Marine Corps mentality, battle scars are badges of merit. They are the medals of heroes. Parents have related to me that it was their religious faith that sustained them when the professionals said,

"We can do no more." Their children are still dependent, but the family has done what could be done, and life must go on. How much easier it must be when you feel that God approves and is with you.

In his discussion of faith, Eugene McDonald (16) made several good points about parents and their religious beliefs. They are:

1. Parental religious beliefs can have a definite influence on their child's habilitation program.
2. Parental religious beliefs should not interfere with a handicapped child's habilitation services.
3. Parents should not allow their religious beliefs to interfere with the carrying out of their personal responsibilities.
4. Their religious commitment fills many of the needs of parents of handicapped children.

These statements appear to violate the parent's rights to exercising his religious beliefs. These statements might apply when they are concerned with the parent's own problems or handicaps. Some feel that the child should be given his chance, even if he is too young to voice his own feelings.

Parents will benefit from their religion only if they use it to find strength and wisdom needed to understand and manage their problems.

A parent's religious beliefs can also present problems to their child's habilitation program. It becomes a detriment when they use those beliefs as a temporary refuge in which to escape temporarily from their problems. It is not good to escape into church work and religious counseling to the point that the child comes second to the pursuit of religious knowledge. We have seen a few parents take this route, searching for God's meaning. Without meaning, life becomes intolerable. It is common for all of us to struggle with the meaning of troublesome events in our lives. In the event of a handicapped child, the struggle is more futile, yet the solutions are vastly more important. We must grieve appropriately for a while, then pick up the pieces and move on.

To a degree, the amount of loss felt over a handicapped child can relate to the amount of personal lifestyle lost. A person who had very little life outside of the home would feel less loss than one who was actively involved with career and community. What is to be changed and why? That is an important question when it comes to finding meaning. Will the handicapped child affect bowling, shopping, club meetings, exercise classes, etc.? These are very basic questions to be answered. These questions never enter some parents' minds. To others, however, they are very real concerns and should not be overlooked. Loss of these activities would add a whole new meaning to their grief and their lives.

Usually, you will find parents looking much deeper than their own satisfactions for a new meaning to their lives. Some will be pursuing possibilities for new philosophies. Some will search for a better way to live. Others will be agonizing over the loss of the previous meaning that their life had.

Perhaps the one thing that hinders some parents' recovery from grief is that this incident has no place at all in the created order of their universe. It is completely alien to their way of thinking. Intellectually, they can admit that these things do happen in the universe, but emotionally, they have assumed that it would never happen to them or their loved ones. The illusion that they are the exception to the rule prevents them from devoting themselves to anything but the internal argument against this intrusion into their lives. They are tempted to make a "vocation" of grief. It is true that some people get more attention and sympathy during this time than they have had at any other time in their life. For some it is tempting to hang on to that attention and glory in it. It is a good feeling to feel "cared for." We live in a society of instant fix. People believe that the best way to help their children is to fix the problem immediately. By the same token, when they, themselves, run into a problem, they want it fixed. If said problem cannot be fixed, the search for meaning can be a long, hard one.

You, as a people who are involved with handicapped children, cannot provide an instant fix. The future meaning of parents with handicapped children must be determined by the parents of the child. We have no right to criticize the meaning that another person may develop during their search. We as parents, friends, and relatives can sympathize and provide understanding to those who are constructing a new life that they can live with.

Chapter 8

A Calling and a Recommitment to Life

When a parent has found a new meaning to life, they will follow a plan of recommitting to life. Feelings and ideals have come together, and the parent or parents have decided where they want to go with their lives. They may have decided to devote their lives to development of this special child. They may even decide to work for all special children and become involved in activities with rehabilitation agencies, special education classes, and special olympics. Whatever they decide to do, they need to establish a plan. To enter into these endeavors without a plan only brings confusion and grief. We have often seen one parent decide to take this route without the consideration of the other parent or the other children in the family. This is a bad plan.

To develop a good plan, it is well to remember that this is a new and confusing set of circumstances that you are in. Do you know what you are doing? Probably not. So, what we need first is information with which to make a plan. To do so, we will need to talk to rehabilitation people and find out what is needed to help your child. Is it equipment, books, funding, or leadership from parent groups? If you ask, you will get enough information to get started.

At a center where I worked, we had the funding, and we had the equipment. Our staff was well trained and doing their jobs. When a parent wanted to help, the only project that came immediately to mind was a "professional library" for the staff and parents. Boy, did we open a floodgate. It was wonderful. Within a short time, these folks had a city library, three university libraries, and the medical library of an out-of-state university making recommendations of what literature was needed and what was available. These folks had a new calling and commitment to life. By the end of the year, the library was outstanding, and they were involved in projects to help the public schools with their special education programs. The local special education department became one of the best equipped in the state. All it took was a plan.

There is a hazard involved with people who become too devoted to the service of handicapped children. It is easy, in their enthusiasm, to get carried away. It is good for the receiving agency and the kids involved, but other important elements in life can be neglected. We have seen families fall apart when one parent becomes too absorbed in the process.

Wolfelt (24) cautions, "We often have inappropriate expectations of how well we should be doing." He points out that we are told to "carry on," "keep your chin up," and "keep busy." In actuality we need to slow down, turn inward, and embrace our feelings. So, it makes more sense to "take your time," "do a good job," and "take one step at a time." Accepting your child's condition is just the first of several levels of acceptance. You also need to accept your own limitations, accept that the husband or wife still needs you and that other children in the family need you.

Some parents will center their attention on the normal children in the family to assist them in leading a normal life rather than carry the stigma of having an abnormal family. This is not a good plan. When you are trying to hide the fact that there is an abnormal person in the family, how do you do it? First, you keep people out of your house so that they won't see the child. This means that the children cannot bring their friends home with them. Bad plan. This in itself marks the family as abnormal. This is exactly what you are trying to avoid.

Often, we see one parent centering on the normal children. Another bad plan. This divides the family and creates many more problems than it solves. When creating a plan, it is always a good idea to consider the problems that the plan can create. You may just be trading one set of problems for another. Take time to consider the consequences of what you are about to do.

When planning their new lives, it is easy for parents to oversimplify. They decide what the child means to them and what they are going to do for him. Then, they go wholeheartedly into the plan. If that plan does not work, then they suffer further grief, anxiety, and guilt. Parents need to get help with their plan. Don't just sit down and say, "Here's what we're going to do." Consult with other parents and see how they handle it. Talk to social workers. They are the greatest source of information that you may find. They are involved with the whole family and the agencies that may benefit it in this time of need.

At one time in my career, I directed a pilot project to do research into how we could help infants up to three years of age. Up to that point, we had taken them when they turned three. Our center had a social worker who served pretty much as an admissions clerk. I thought that was her job. I didn't even know, back then, what a social worker was. One day she asked me why I did not include a social worker on my staff. Being somewhat taken aback, I sat down and said, "Tell me what you can do for my kids." For the next thirty minutes she talked fast. By the time we were through that day, I had convinced the center director that I had to have her on my staff.

It was a great move. That unhappy lady, who was very upset about being made an admissions clerk, put a smile on her face and did what she was trained to do. It was truly an "eye opening," beautiful situation. She helped so many parents over the rough spots by helping them to make viable—plans for getting through their grief, plans for providing the best services for their child, and plans for keeping the family on track. When help was needed, everyone turned to her. She was truly in her glory. I would never attempt another project like that without a social worker on board.

One thing our social worker taught our parents was not to stop with plan A. You need plan B and C, just in case. Any game plan can go awry at times.

If a plan does not have complete approval, failure is almost imminent. We must include every member of the family, big or small, in the plan.

If a child is too small to participate in the planning, we must plan for him. We must keep in mind, as mentioned before, this experience does not fit into the family's expectations and hopes. They are in a whole new universe, and the probability of errors is monumental. Just by pointing out the hazards, we have been able to help some families adjust and make a smooth transition.

With the defeat of some hopes, new hopes arise. Gone are the hopes of normalcy, and now the hope for near normalcy prevails. We hope for happiness, physical mobility, education, and self-sufficiency.

How do we handle the changing hopes in our lives? Very little has been written on the subject of parents with handicapped children rebuilding their lives. The information that we have found in the research of the grief process is written about those who have suffered through the death of a loved one. There is good information for those who have suffered loss through divorce. I even found a book on how to handle the grief over the loss of a pet. When it comes to a handicapped child, however, the information is scarce.

There are some obvious differences noted right away. For one thing, the person who has lost another person has to go on without that person. They rebuild their life around a void. With a handicapped child, we have lost the child that we expected, but instead of a void, there is a whole new dimension complete with multiple problems to be dealt with. There is not a problem of doing without, but, instead, the problem of doing with. Remember, you have suffered the death of a dream. Don't forget what you wanted; just recognize what you got.

While some hopes have died, other hopes arise. It is not uncommon, however, to have parents who can tell about the hopes that they had for their child. They hoped for that perfect child who would be of good nature, pleasant to look at, and popular with other people. They hope for a good education, a good marriage, and a glowing career. There is the distant hope of grandchildren. But, what do parents hope for their child with disabilities? Most say that they hope he can achieve his potential. There is a big difference when talking about hope for normal and abnormal. We need to change that. Parents need to "hope" for their child, no matter what station he may achieve in life.

To have hopes, we must have fantasies. Let your mind wander and consider the prospects and possibilities. Over the years I have come up with some fantastic memories. My memories are good because someone else had hopes and fantasies. I remember the man in the wheelchair who maintained twenty-one vehicles for a rehabilitation center as well as running a prefabrication shop that designed and built much of the equipment for the babies that I worked with. I remember him driving his motor home, equipped with hand controls that he had designed and built. He also drove the trucks and tractors that he had on his small stock farm. He was asked one time, "How do you see yourself as different from Ben?" He said, "Well, Ben wears out a lot of boots, and I wear out a lot of tires." He was so versatile that we often forgot he was in a wheelchair. I once caught myself fussing at him because he didn't take his wife dancing. Duh!

I remember a severely cerebral palsied man who walked on his toes and talked with typical c.p. writhing speech. He was CEO of seven corporations and got about in a Learjet. I remember a blind boy who worked and bought his own car. (He only dated girls who had a driver's license.) He was also a bull rider in the high school rodeo, which is a big deal in Texas. When teased about that "dog" he was out with on Saturday night, he laughed and said, "I know what she looked like. I have it all over you guys. I can only see by "feel." I could go on about the wonderful people that I know who have disabilities, but I think the point is made. We must have hope, fantasy, and a plan. Most children adopt the philosophy of the parents. Most successful people with disabilities say, "I was taught to work with what I got." If the parents are OK, the kid will be OK.

When plans are made, each person must have a "role." If the plan includes a role for the mom, a role for the dad, and a role for each sibling, things don't get so complicated. Most siblings adapt and feel good about themselves if they have a role in the family. It makes them part of a very important project. A role, no matter how simple or complicated, helps people to be in control. With control comes more comfort, satisfaction, and happiness.

You should also consider the roles of those outside the family. Don't exclude those who had a role in your life before. They may be separated by your tragedy. Pull them back into your life and define the role that they play in your life. They'll love you for it.

The recommitment to life is not a superficial quick fix. It's the real thing. It is thought through, planned, and implemented with purpose. It is the start of your new life.

Chapter 9

The Struggle Not to Abandon Loved Ones

Unfortunately, we have seen some cases where the family abandoned the handicapped child. Does that sound unbelievable? To a parent who truly loves his child, that is unthinkable. But, sadly, it happens. When all thoughts are hopeless and nothing makes sense, the idea of an institution surfaces. There are some cases where this may be appropriate. When parents are unable to provide for their child at home and the child's needs are so extensive that they are completely beyond their means, some parents let go and put the child in an institution where he will receive medical help, everyday care, and some education. It is hard on some parents that have made that decision even when it was the right thing to do. When the family is able to face the facts and make the institution decision, there is nearly always a certain amount of grief and guilt. They feel inadequate and they feel that they have let their child down.

In some cases, we have seen some members of a family withdraw and leave all tasks associated with the handicapped child to other members of the family. Mothers often say that they have been abandoned because the dad goes to work, kids go to school, and the mom stays home to take care of the new baby. Even if this is not totally true, it may be perceived in that light. The loneliness of everyday tasks and the isolation from the family, even for short periods, may lead to these self-centered thoughts.

When siblings were not included in the plan, they often felt abandoned themselves. They went on to make their life meaningful with their friends, never acknowledging that there was a new brother or sister. While the mom takes care of things at home, the other children virtually raise themselves. When they take this route, they usually abandon the rest of the family and go on alone or with friends. Sure, they eat and sleep at home, but they do not feel like part of the family.

Occasionally, we see a whole family split up under these same circumstances. The dad goes to work, the brother goes to school and hangs out with his friends, and the sister spends her time with her friends, usually at their house. That leaves the mom at home, alone, with the handicapped child. As doctor appointments, rehabilitation appointments, parent groups, etc., take more and more of her time, she may even like the idea of not having to provide for the rest of the family. She may appreciate that the kids have a safe place to go.

On the other hand, when a family sticks together and sends the handicapped child to an M.R. facility, rehabilitation facility, nursing home, or state school, it is easy to drift away and never visit or care for the severely disabled individual. Often, they do not pay expenses or anything else. At this point the agencies become a "warehouse" for the unwanted.

It is easy for outsiders to judge people in the situation described above. Society often judges them harshly, but in reality, their coping skills have failed, their energies have become exhausted, and their judgment may have become impaired. They may have nothing left with which to operate. Their whole working system grinds to a halt. They may go on with life, but they are never the same. Shame and guilt may always be there.

In cases where a handicapped individual has been abandoned, it is not just that individual who has lost. The whole family has lost. Every member of that family needs support, affection, and relief from despair. As I once noted, "It is not just the child who is handicapped. It is the whole family." In some cases, the handicapped child may be the only one who gets care. He may not even be aware of the family situation. Those who are left at home, with awareness, are the ones who suffer.

There are actually some individuals who bolt and run in these circumstances. They leave the rest of the family to bear the load. In most of these cases, we see the man doing the deserting. With dreams crushed, expenses piling up, and no relief in sight, some people are just not tough enough. They break and run. If found and confronted, the man will nearly always relate the problem to finances. They are just not able to face the future with no prospect of coming out on top financially. They literally go and start over somewhere else.

Some men have related their actions to embarrassment and their loss of manhood. They often say that the wife has deserted them to take care of the kid. There is no partnership involved anymore. There is no sex; after all, that's how this whole thing started. Men who run in the face of inferiority feelings were surely confronted with these same problems before the birth of their child. The child just added the "straw that broke the camel's back." In some cases we have seen mothers who deserted the family. Their reasons are different from the fathers' in that they usually relate to the impossibility of accepting the "role" assigned to them as "lone" and "total" caregiver of the handicapped child for the rest of his life. Rather than try to work something out where they would not have to assume that role, they just panic and run. It is interesting to note that many more of them return to assume their responsibility than do fathers. Temporary insanity does happen.

Another problem that may emerge is the sibling who runs away from home. They just cannot stand the turmoil and disruption in their life, so they leave. This compounds the family's grief at a time when they are already overloaded. In some instances, we have seen whole families come apart because one of the normal children could not accept the stigma of the handicapped child or felt that they were pushed aside, so they ran. Now the family is torn between caring for the handicapped child and worrying about the safety of the runaway. You see total destruction on every side.

Where does a family turn in such a time of torment? Is there anything available to help them survive? It is often not enough for parents to try to support each other. You must keep in mind that this may be the first experience of this kind for the family. If you are not aware of the different agencies that have been created to help grieving parents, then you may miss their benefit. The Family Service Organization is one group that has a national program for family care. It has centers all over the United States. These centers are supported by United Way, United Fund, or Community Chest funds. They offer good programs that assist families in need of guidance, support, and care. If such agencies are not listed locally, then call the nearest medical facility and ask for help in locating them. A talk with a hospital chaplain, the head of family services or the head of the department of psychiatry can often point a family in the right direction. As I mentioned in the previous chapter, if there is a rehabilitation center near, talk to the social worker. There is a way to get help and support. It is his job to see that people in need get the help they ask for.

It is my firm belief that by rehabilitating the whole family, we can provide better service to people with disabilities. I encourage all families to present their situation and ask how they can get family therapy in their crisis.

Let's suppose that you are in a great financial position. The cost of services is no problem. The mom is a stay-at-home mom, so there is no disruption of her career. There should really be no problem in providing the care that the new baby needs. Are all of the problems solved? Not hardly. As listed above, there are many emotional issues that arise. There are personal feelings involved. There are too many unanswered questions.

In my own situation, I made it a practice to pursue families. Once I learned that they were covering up their feelings and putting up a front, I made it a point to send all parents to our social worker at least once or twice while I worked with their child. She was excellent at pulling information from them and guiding them to the right spot to get the answers that needed to be answered.

A family need not live with the memory of having abandoned a handicapped loved one. Even if that person is better off in an institution, knowing that he or she has a caring family adds a happy dimension to their lives. With proper care and guidance, you can work through your problems, not out of them. Some of my fondest memories over the years have been in seeing a family "get it together" and become a strong, functioning group. What a pleasure it is to see other children respond and accept their handicapped siblings as a meaningful member of the family. This in itself gives parents a new insight into their children and into their family unit.

I have seen children grow and become strong individuals. I have seen older children working as volunteers in summer programs at rehabilitation centers and special schools. The experience is beautiful in that they find themselves being truly useful and appreciated for the first time. A look of appreciation and a hug is very meaningful, especially when it comes from a child with disabilities. Their perspective on life led them on to greater things. So many of our good professionals today come up through the ranks of the volunteers. Through their experience and service, they become acquainted with outstanding occupations and careers that they might never have known otherwise.

Don't make the mistake of letting your family slip through the cracks. Make it a point to search out information that is available that will help your family to adjust and thrive. If you start in the beginning, your family will be less likely to self-destruct.

At one time in my career, I worked as a director of special education for an education service center. It was a big mistake. I realized that I had reached my level of incompetence. I stuck to that job for a year out of pure hardheadedness. I realized that I was not an administrator; I was a therapist. So I quit my high-paying job and went back to being myself. But, one day, while I was special education director, my boss came to me and told me about a family who had a severely retarded, ten-year-old girl who was large for her age. She was a "screamer" and occasionally had to be restrained because of her tendency to be a "head banger" when she was upset, which was often. He described the mom as calm, never smiling, doing her job of taking care of the child faithfully. Lately, the mother demonstrated a tendency to cry quietly while alone. She had also developed a tic on her right cheek and eye. He described the father as a professional man with multiple degrees and a tendency to stay at the office and work late hours. Two teenage brothers were good students and athletes but stayed away from home as much as possible. "What," he asked, "would you recommend?" I advised him that I could not make a recommendation without seeing the situation firsthand, but it did sound like more care might be needed for the child than the mother was capable of giving. He then asked, "Would you come to my house this evening and visit?" During my visit, I got a chance to see the family together. The father had requested that the two boys stay home for the evening long enough to meet me. They were good-looking kids who were polite and answered my questions honestly. No, they did not like being at home. No, they did not bring their friends around, and, no, they did not want anyone to see their sister. They were obviously anxious to leave but were polite enough to stay. They nearly ran over me getting out of the driveway as I was leaving.

During the visit, the mother appeared to be in control, but the tic in her right eye and cheek were very noticeable. During that hour, she had to stop the daughter from head banging two times. The child became upset for no apparent reason. During that time, she screamed loudly twelve times. Each time the father closed his eyes and clenched his teeth momentarily and then went on as if nothing had happened.

The next day, I visited with the father and asked why they had not considered an institution. He said, "We considered it, but they have long waiting lists, and we just didn't pursue it." I knew of a state school that accepted some children on an "emergency" basis for thirty days. If the situation were critical enough, they would keep the child after that. I made a phone call and described what I had seen. The director said, "Bring 'er on." My boss sat there with tears in his eyes and agreed to go. Later, he told me about the trip. The daughter had fussed a little about being left but settled down when they told her that this was her new school. He said, "We could have cheerfully cut our throats on the way home." According to the rules, they could not visit during the first thirty days. This was to give the child a chance to settle down and adjust to her new life.

Two weeks later, while en route to a doctor's appointment, the husband and wife had to drive through the town where the state school was located. The wife was anxious to know how the daughter was doing, so they stopped and called. They understood that they couldn't visit but inquired as to how she was adjusting. The psychologist said that she was doing great and that they could visit if they wanted to. The daughter's adjustment had been remarkable.

The visit was brief, and the daughter appeared happy to see them. They visited and had a great time. The psychologist reported that the head banging was no longer evident, and she screamed only when she was really upset, usually once or twice a day.

When they got ready to leave, they thought they had made a big mistake. The daughter became agitated, but the psychologist explained, "Oh no, you're not going. You are going to stay at school. Mommy and Daddy are going home now." Then the daughter smiled and waved "bye bye." This was a case where institutionalization was a must. The daughter was happy, the family recovered, and all was well on the home front. The last time I saw the mother, she had come by the service center to visit. She had a new hairstyle, was stylishly dressed, and looked relaxed. We all enjoyed her visit that day. Our director, the father of the previously mentioned child, was a new man. He could hardly wait to get out the door and get home in the evening. He was relaxed, smiling, and enjoying life once again.

In this case, the daughter was not abandoned. The family visits often, and she is always happy to see them. Two years later, there was no head banging and no screaming.

Whatever your case may be, get the help to do the right thing for your child and for your family. As the famous Western writer, Louis L'Amour said, "When you think it is the end, it is just the beginning."

Chapter 10

The Inner Struggle

During the parent's time of grief over a handicapped child, he will have many inner struggles. Of all of those struggles that go on, the ones mentioned most often are the ones of rage, despair, and bitterness. Studies in other areas of psychology will often point out that these phenomena are the ones that are most likely to eat away at a person, and by that nature, they are the ones that are most likely to incapacitate the individual. How can a person react meaningfully to those about him when inside he is feeling that powerful rage that makes him want to lash out and destroy something? How does he overcome that feeling of hopelessness and despair long enough to do something creative and meaningful in his life or the lives of those who share his life? How does a person function in an optimistic way when the overwhelming feelings of bitterness are eating away at him and are the uppermost feelings in his consciousness?

Feelings of rage are usually the result of people's feelings of injustice and frustration over their best efforts to cope with their hopes for their loved ones. They may, in their frustration think, "Why don't they die?" Then, they suffer those pangs of guilt that are associated with such thoughts. Some parents, in therapy, have even stated that they even had thoughts of killing the child to end his misery or to end the prospect of a lifetime of what they were feeling at that time. They fear losing control of this rage.

With all of these feelings comes a feeling of worthlessness that further inhibits the healing process. In some cases, this feeling and this period in their life is the absolute bottom.

If a person is able to express these feelings, they are on the road to overcoming them. To solve a problem, we must first acknowledge it. When this admission takes place, they want to do something about it. That, in itself, is the first step forward. It is at times like this that I assure folks that they are certainly not the first to have these thoughts, and this too is part of the grief process. While it is not the best solution, it is still natural to want to remove this heavy burden from someone that you care about. We just need another plan. We have a problem that can be handled and overcome. It is a time to work through the problem, find an acceptable solution, and move on to the resolution of that problem.

Some people state that they have a strong feeling of despair when rage overtakes them. They have had some times during their life when they got mad, really mad. They state, "This is different. When I was mad before, there was someone to blame, even if it was myself." They were able to rationalize their way through their feelings of being mad, or they could just walk away from the situation and let their madness work itself out in time. That prospect is not available when they are faced with a handicapped child who will be with them as long as one or the other remains alive. This is a never-ending thing.

Some parents have reported that they tend to take out their rage on themselves while others report that they take it out on other family members who are more able to defend themselves. At these times, they will fall asleep at night knowing that they face a new day tomorrow that looks harsh, bleak, and uninviting. They have lost their desire for food. They have lost their sexual desire for their partner. They have lost interest in their family, their hobbies, their favorite TV shows, and all else in their life. They are tired and all they have to think about is "more of the same" in the years to come. They report that they drag themselves through each essential task. They neglect those tasks which they consider unessential. "What do we do now?" they ask.

It is time to reach out for medical help and counseling. When a person has reached this all-time low, it is time for expert help. Counseling in itself may not be enough. There may be a strong enough need for a crutch such as medication to help stabilize things while you have a chance to work through these personal problems. They are personal at this point because the thoughts and feelings are coming from within. It is time for a psychiatrist. This suggestion may be met with resistance as psychiatric help is expensive, and the financial burden faced with the handicapped child has already contributed to those feelings of despair. But, in the long run, it may be one of the most beneficial expenses incurred.

It is a time to band together with others who are understanding and helpful. It is a time to work with those who understand and are not condemning. It's time for good doctors, psychologists, social workers, and friends. Preferably, the friends are those new friends that also have handicapped children. They have been down your path, and they know what you are going through.

Shafts of light will soon begin to appear and the end of despair is in sight. Count on it.

Closely associated with despair is a strong feeling of bitterness. Again and again, parents ask the question, "Why is God punishing me this way?" They may begin to feel bitterness toward God and others in their lives. It is not uncommon for us to see one of the family searching the background of the other family members to determine if that is where the "bad genes" came from. So many parents have brought these thoughts and feelings to the surface with the remark "Nothing like this has ever happened in my family before." They are not talking about the family that they have created. They are wondering about the spouse's gene pool.

Perpetual sorrow is not the only provocation of bitterness. Nevertheless, it deserves close attention. This struggle against bitterness is perpetual and usually never completely won. With each disappointment through time and the life span of this special child, there will be bitterness.

At times, bitterness can lead to a set of plans to get even, to retaliate. It is at these times that we have seen drastic changes in people's behavior patterns.

How often we have seen a mother, consumed with bitterness and a loss of sexual desire for her husband, turn away from that sexual contact. This will be discussed further in the next chapter dealing with marital distancing. You might feel that it was sex that brought this whole thing on, or you might feel that this could happen again. In this situation of confused thinking and bitterness, it is not surprising to see parents withdraw from each other. On another level, it is also a way of getting even. It becomes a punishing behavior. This pattern of willful behavior comes into being that can only set up a vicious circle of retaliation, one toward the other. When this happens, the other partner, going through the same feelings will, more than likely, get even.

When that behavior is established, we often see the husband withdraw into his work, further complicating an already complicated situation. At worse, we see the husband turn to another woman for his sexual needs, creating still more complications than the family can possibly survive. In these situations, the family will often break up. This is really a time when parents need to cling together, supporting each other and giving what comfort they can. They should band together with each other and their children.

In these experiences, we have found that the critical problem is that people are willing to put severe experiences at the center of their whole life. Anything besides love that is placed at the center of your life begins to exercise demonic, possessive power over you. We are in effect, consumed with it. How hard it is to show someone with such severe problems that love is their only possible salvation. They must love God—if they are of religious nature—their spouse, their children, and especially their handicapped child with enough intensity to do the right thing at the right time. It is a time to give each his due and his forgiveness for real or imagined sins. It is a time to embrace friendships and care for those who care for you.

With years of experience in dealing with families and handicapped children, I have come to feel that relations with others can be the most critical issue in overcoming the problems of a handicapped child. The child will draw on the family for his own feelings and attitudes as he develops. This is especially true in areas of love and acceptance within the family. Family attitudes will set his whole tone of development for the future. It is with this in mind that a whole chapter has been devoted to marital distancing.

Chapter 11

The Struggle of Marital Distancing

Dealing with the problems of a handicapped child can, in many ways, be overpowering. Due to the uniqueness of the problems presented, everything is literally blown out of proportion. Added to this is the fact that each problem of the child's adds to and compounds the problems of the parents. Everything becomes bigger than life itself. The family is not just facing hundreds of new problems; they are facing super problems. Some parents report that they feel like they are looking at everything through a magnifying glass.

By now, you have noticed the repetitive nature of this book. It is so because of the repetitive nature of the grief process involved with a "special" child. It is never just "Oh, I have a handicapped child, and it hurt." It is pain over and over. There is pain over the loss of a dream and the pain of seeing your child struggle to master the tasks of life. There is pain over the loss of personal freedom and about the financial strain. There are so many milestones of development, and your child will suffer through each one. Again, you will feel the pain of each.

To pull away from pain is a natural thing. We also have a fear of the unknown, so we draw back in anticipation of what is to come. Will we succeed in accomplishing developmental tasks on time? Will we ever be able to achieve that success of walking, talking, going to school? I think we have a built-in safety factor in our very being that is designed to pull away from what might hurt us. It is only natural for parents to pull away from each other at times like these. That unknown factor of what the other person is thinking and doing causes doubts.

Because each person grieves differently, he may feel that the other's grief is not as deep or that the other is not as "hurt" as he is himself. In such cases, the selfishness mentioned before plays a strong role. We nearly always feel that we have better insight into problems or that we feel things more strongly than do other people.

One day, while standing in my backyard, I heard glass breaking in my neighbor's yard. I didn't pay much attention at first, but it happened again and again. Finally, I looked over the fence to see what was going on. Bob (not his real name) was sitting on the picnic table staring off into space. He was drinking beer, and as he finished each one he threw the bottle against the brick wall of the garage. Well, I'm a curious sort of guy, so I got my six-pack and went over to join him. He didn't speak, so I sat with him, drinking beer and throwing bottles against the wall.

When the last bottle was thrown, I asked Bob what we were celebrating. With tears rolling down his cheeks, he told me that his wife had taken their twenty-one-year-old, retarded daughter to place her in a halfway house where she would have a life of her own. Then, his wife was going on to Maryland to visit with her folks for a couple of weeks' vacation. He looked at me through the tears and said, "I wasn't invited." As Bob's story unfolded, it became evident that his wife had taken care of their daughter for twenty-one years. The halfway house placement was somewhat akin to a normal child going off to college. She was going out on her own, so to speak. The two of them had taken vacations every year to see the grandparents while Bob stayed home and worked. I asked him what he did with his vacations. He said, "I've never had one." I asked him what his wife had to say about it, and he said, "We've never discussed it." I asked, "Why not?" "It just never came up, and I didn't know how to bring it up," he replied.

We sat there for some time, talking and watching the sun go down. It was a classic case of the mom devoting herself to the child while the dad devoted himself to paying for everything. They both did their jobs well for twenty-one years, just not together.

When Bob started to clean up the mess, I had an idea. I told him, "Leave it. When she asks what that was about, tell her." It was about three weeks later that I again heard broken glass tinkling in the backyard of my neighbor. When I looked over the fence, Bob's wife was picking up the glass and putting it into a cardboard box. I went over to help. When she looked at me, there was pain in her eyes. Tears streamed down her face, and she said, "I never knew. He was dying inside, and I never knew." By nature of our society, men tend to lose themselves in work and grieve inwardly. Most men don't weep or show their anger as readily as do women. Men may feel the responsibility of providing a strong shoulder for the wife to lean on and in turn can't lean on the wife during this critical time. He may be very angry, but how many times in his life was he told, "No talking back, no slamming doors, no foot stomping, go to bed, apologize, or get that ugly look off of your face" ? That does not exactly teach a person to investigate, understand, and express feelings of anger. Stearns (21), in her book, points out that "unfortunately, our society continues to place cruel expectations upon men when it comes to the true expression of emotion. No sorrow, guilt, anger, hopelessness, or fear." It can't be put in any better language than that.

Just as parents expect a child to fulfill a role in their lives, men expect wives to fulfill a role in theirs. Wives also expect husbands to love, protect, and provide for them. When the child and the wife both fail in those expectations, deprivation sets in and then grief. In an effort to propagate the species, God or Nature, as the case may be, made men the aggressor in sexual matters. The sex drive is usually stronger in the male, and thus his problems are compounded when the wife withdraws. Some women just don't understand how a man can think of such things at a time like this.

The marital distancing syndrome is a real troublesome thing. Whether it centers around sex, finances, family control, or whatever, it creates problems that make solutions more and more difficult. On the other hand, wives may feel that everything should be put on the back burner until the "real" problems are solved. With a handicapped child, that means never. There will always be problems.

As strange as it may seem, some men have described their need for sex, following a traumatic event as a need to hang on to someone. They say, "It was not about sexual satisfaction. It was about a need to just hold someone and hang on." One man in our study said, "I just needed to be held. She thinks I'm after sex anytime I hug her." Sex is part of life, and so it is with grief. One thing is for sure, if sex was part of the relationship, it will surely be part of the grief.

Our society has also assigned the financial burden to men. In these later years, we have seen two family incomes, single working moms, and even househusbands. Typically, however, it is the man who has the most responsibility when it comes to finances. People generally do not like to talk about their finances, but it is very unusual to meet a family who does not feel the financial stress when it comes to having a handicapped child. It can cause more problems when there is not enough money to go around. It makes some men feel inadequate. It makes some women blame their husbands for not being a better provider.

Nature and society have also been unreasonable in assigning women the task of nurturing and caring for the young. Therefore, she is designated the major responsibility of caring for the handicapped child. It is normal for that child to take up her time and effort to the exclusion of all else. Burdened with this responsibility, it is only natural for her to withdraw into the task. After a day of taking care of an un-potty trained youngster who is constantly drooling, has to be spoon-fed, and cared for in every way, she may be just a little tired and disgusted. Not only is she expected to do that, but also she is expected to take care of herself, the house, the other children, and her husband. After all, what has she done besides get her husband off to work, the kids off to school, cook, care for the new baby, take him to the rehabilitation center, have conferences with the professional staff, try to remember medications and home treatments, and try to look appealing for her husband when he comes home from work. Is it any wonder that she might withdraw just a little bit or fall into bed at night worried about the possibility of how many times she may have to get up with the kids during the night? It is indeed a miracle when such a super mom does not withdraw.

It is not unusual for a mother to turn her total attention to nursing the handicapped child. When she does this, she in effect cuts the bond with the father. At this point, she may come to lean on her friends, her pastor, or the professional staff that is attending to the child's rehabilitation. One mother put it this way, "Any time I lean on him, he grabs me and heads for the bedroom." At the same time, it might be that the father wants none of this. He may feel confused about the amount of time she is spending with others. He may rationalize that she has to spend a lot of time with the child, and that is alright. But does she have to spend the rest of her time with everybody else? Already feeling deprived, a father can get in further trouble by confronting his wife with his need for her to spend more time taking care of him.

It is essential for parents to communicate with each other in terms of their grief. If one has not expressed his feelings, the other should take note and pursue that information. It is important to have everyone's feelings on the table. They need to understand that each has a different way of grieving and a different way of expressing that grief.

If the situation is that the mother is neglecting everything else to care for her child, this should give the father a clue that changes need to be made on his end. The wife should have the opportunity to do other things in the same way that the father has. She needs to gain some respite from the strain. Respite can be a very valuable thing in these hard times. Some institutions have acknowledged this great need and have arranged for emergency respite care for the handicapped child, just so the parents have a chance to get away, regroup, and survive.

Survival becomes the name of the game in most families who have a severely handicapped child. Anything that can be done to help them in that survival mode is a legitimate endeavor.

To accomplish survival, each parent must look at each other's darkest feelings and develop a balanced perspective. With that balanced perspective, if they are lucky, they will be able to put the rest of the world in its proper place and go forward with the task at hand.

Chapter 12

Grieving but Staying Well

With a child on our hands who has special needs, it is our job to help that child in every way possible. McDonald (16), in his book, has pointed out that a child does not exist in isolation but as part of a family. It is not enough for us to treat the child's problems and disregard the family's needs and feelings. In a very real sense, we never have just a handicapped child, rather a handicapped family.

Stearns (21) has pointed out that the first significant studies in America began in early 1940 on human psychology and how it pertains to grief. Only in the last two generations have scientists gathered systematic information about the processes of human adjustment pertaining to bereavement. Most of these studies have related to death and dying. Very little has been said about the handicapped child. A child with special needs presents more problems to the parents in that there is no end in sight and their grief is a never-ending thing. It is with this in mind that we must make attempts to heal the whole family and help each member with their adjustment to this tragedy.

If you want firsthand knowledge into the confusion that a family might be going through and to experience some similar confusion, try reading an insurance policy and gain an understanding without an agent to guide you. You will, again, meet frustration head on. This is much the same thing as trying to find the information you need about a child who has problems, what those problems are, how to handle the problems, and insure the health of the family in the process. The jargon used in the literature and that of the professional people involved can be very confusing.

Taking a lead from Krumroy (9), in her book "Grief is Not Forever," we have found it helpful to those in grief to just say, "I'll stick with you the best I can." Many parents have said that these words have meant more to them than anything else. It conveys the message that we may not fully understand your pain and grief, but we are with you anyway. It will not be easy on friends and other family because they are not usually prepared for what comes. Our society has neglected the needs of the family because everyone was conditioned to look at the child's problems and concentrate on what needed to be done. We were looking at the medical aspects first, and it took a long time for the psychological problems to surface and be recognized. Again, this may be due to the fact that parents have been so good about putting on a brave face and doing what needed to be done without voicing their own injury.

The process that parents go through with handicapped children often follows the same course that we see when there is a child who dies or is in the process of dying. We have taken our lead from that literature because there has been very little written about the grief process that takes place over the child with special needs. Again and again, we have seen in the literature that the family grieves and needs to be helped. Yet, there have been very few suggestions as to what we as individuals can do to help each other. Based on the mentioned literature and our experience, I have tried to put down some meaningful suggestions that will help.

You must feel good enough about yourself to talk to other people and counselors about your feelings and concerns. You must listen to other family members and accept their feelings. If you don't care for or like their feelings, remember, those feelings belong to them just as yours belong to you. Also remember, they will change from time to time. Many listeners are very uncomfortable listening to another person's feelings. It often brings forth painful feelings of your own. But, keep a level head and respond as both friend and family member, or bystander. Aside from being good listeners and talkers on our own behalf, we must pursue information and educate friends and family about what is going on. Knowledge nearly always smoothes the path that a person has to travel. At times, it is enough to tell that person that they are following a normal course that will awaken them to the prospects of what is to come and assure them that everything is going on schedule.

We must as parents, partners, and friends pause to care, to share, to listen, to feel, and to respond to each other. We must try to remain healthy amid confusion, anger, hostility, stress, and grief.

Family needs will change from the onset of the handicapping condition and continue in many forms until long after death has occurred either to the child or to the other family members. It is for this reason that family members should handle their energy economically and not exert themselves to the point that they collapse when they are needed most. Even after the child is taken care of, the family must go on. They often do not know who to talk to, and the professionals involved are so busy they do not make themselves available. I remember the days when I had therapy treatments scheduled back to back every thirty minutes, all day long. It doesn't give you time to think about anything except the immediate needs of the child. In the end, parents and family members are lucky if they find someone who is available to talk and listen to their concerns. That is why I have recommended that all programs have a social worker who can be actively involved with families.

Stearns (21) has pointed out that water, as it freezes and the molecules expand, has the power to burst steel pipes wide open. Likewise, frozen emotions assume a power out of proportion to their original nature. During the harsh seasons of grief, it is best to keep the channels open so that hurtful feelings are freely expressed. Because every person and every grief is different, it may be years before the relationships between particular circumstances and particular forms of reaction are worked out to a point where dogmatic statements are possible.

Mourning and grieving are treated by some as if they were a weakness rather than a psychological necessity. We often avoid those who are grieving. This is the time when all people should be involved with those around them. It is very difficult, however, to respond logically to another person, such as a sibling who is in grief, while you are in the same pain. That is why it is so important to get others involved who can listen and accept the feelings expressed. Remember, those who are the most beautiful people in spirit are those who have known defeat, suffering, struggle, and loss yet have found their way out of the depths. Growth can come in unexpected ways from nooks and crannies of our life's experience.

To help other family members, you should try to listen, really listen, to where the other person is coming from. Above all, be sensitive and non-critical of his ever-changing moods. You should, by the same token, be aware of your own changing moods and be willing to discuss them with those around you. By being aware of unresolved anger and guilt and all of the other emotions that go with grief, we can head off the effects that bring forth physical and mental illness. Get it outside the body where it can't eat away at you.

When up against a wall, great anger is usually generated within us. Some people are immediately angry in the face of loss; others seem to wait for their anger to seep in. In either instance, they go through that whole jungle of emotions that need to be expressed in some way. Some people are quick-tempered and fly off the handle quickly and violently, using language that may be shocking. OK, they have expressed it and usually come down from their madness very quickly. Others simmer like a pot of water on low heat, building up for the big explosion. Whatever and however their grief may be, it needs to come out and be dealt with.

To help each other through the grief process, we must first be sure that our information is correct. Here, again, it is best to gather information about a person's anger and grief from that person. If you open the door, he might not immediately pour out all of his anger and grief. But, with the door open, it will eventually begin to escape and be recognized. For those who are on the explaining end, I would suggest that you tell it like it is. Not only will it help you get it off your chest, it will help you and those around you understand where you are in this grief process and also to understand where you need to go with it. Don't brush it off with a lie. Lies have a way of catching up with us, and it is never good to mislead someone who may be hurting with you. Don't say you are OK when you're not.

Let each member of the family know that things are bad, so we feel bad about it. That's OK. Children especially have a way of taking the blame upon themselves when there is a problem in the family. It's almost like it is built into them to do so. Please, if you do nothing else, explain to the kids that something bad has happened, we feel bad about it, and that's normal. It would really be abnormal to feel good about it. It's nobody's fault; it just happened.

It is good to let children in the family, as well as other adults, know that there is a burden to bear and we are going to do it together. Burdens are more easily borne by many, rather than just one.

This is a time to take inventory. Do you have a life support system? Just by identifying the members of the life support system, you relieve part of the burden. It's amazing how many people never call for life support but can relax and enjoy life a little more because they know it is there. Just by taking the step to identify those who are available, you have made a positive step. Every positive step is critical.

How intact is our capacity for empathy with those who seek to comfort us? Just by analyzing that capacity and understanding, it may be another positive step. There may be those who are willing, but you just cannot relate to them. It's good to know. In these cases, you acknowledge that someone is there, but you cannot accept their help.

Once a parent starts asking himself questions about how he is going to get through this, other questions seem to flow out rapidly. Some of the most frequent questions that I have heard are:

1. How long will my child suffer?
2. Will I be able to make the right decisions?
3. What do I do if my child dies?
4. What can I do to make it easier?
5. Should I tell my child what the problem is?
6. Should I tell his siblings what is wrong?

The questions go on and on. At times, the best anyone can do is listen and hope that the right decision will be made. At other times, it may be good to launch out and give advice. Your advice might not be what is needed, but it gives that person a chance to weigh some options. Never take it personally if your suggestion is discarded. You have at least eliminated that one.

Through it all, parents often wonder just what the professional people who work with their child are thinking. Some of the parents in our study put the question to us, and the staff tried to be honest. Here is what they came up with:

1. What is the best way to handle a hysterical person?
2. How do you comfort someone who is suffering from loss better than saying, "I'm sorry" ?
3. How would you know if a person wants help in discussing his grief?
4. If a person is experiencing anger at a loss and displaces this anger on me, what is the best way to handle it?
5. What is the best way to tell someone about the problem of his child if you are the first to know and must relay the message?
6. What can you do when you feel that you've lost the family by distance, personality, or lifestyle changes?
7. Should I let the parent know that I too suffer pain and frustration over the problems that his child suffers?

Perhaps this is just a sample of questions that the professional staff ask themselves, but it does give you the parent a chance to see that they too are just people trying to help you get through this the best they can. In answer to question six, they all agreed that at that point it was time to refer the child on to another therapist. But, it is indeed hard to give up a child once you become attached, even when it's for his own good.

At one point while working with severely handicapped babies, my staff decided we needed some guidance in getting the program under way when a new child came into the program. We had geared up our project thinking that we would possibly have about fifty children who qualified. The qualifying criterion was that they had to have one severe handicap or multiple handicaps. In a short time, we had seen four hundred who qualified. It was staggering. We went through a grief process of our own, then went to work.

We decided that to help parents with their child, we needed to give them as much information as possible to work with. We would lay out the problem, the prognosis, the plan of treatment, and let them know that the program was experimental. We did not know what the outcome would be.

One of the things that we felt was necessary was to be sure that the family understood the terminology that was being used. We simplified where we could but used professional terms when necessary. I had each parent give his own definition of the terms that were most frequently used in our program. Was I amazed! The following definitions came straight from some of the parents:

Anoxia—don't know.
Mental retardation—dumb.
Learning disability—total inability to learn.
Brain damage—bleeding in the head.
Articulation—don't know.
Delayed language—slow speech.

The list goes on and on. What this points out is that we should be very specific about what we believe to be correct. Don't hesitate to ask for explanation of terms and meanings of specific words.

Some parents that we saw were hung up in the denial stage of mourning. They were going from center to center trying to get a different diagnosis. At times it was because they did not want to accept the diagnosis, and at times they did not understand the diagnosis. Always ask for the meaning.

We found that some parents had submerged feelings that kept them from committing to a program. It became necessary to pull information from them. With such information on the table, they began to relate to the problems and work on them. Some of the questions that we asked to help parents discuss their problems were:

When did you first notice that your child had a problem?
What did you think about the problem once you knew what it was?
What is the biggest problem that you face with your child now?
Is there anything or any subject that you would like to talk about?
Are there other problems in the family that might slow things down?
Is there anything else you can think of to talk about?

While details are nearly always different, most families go through the same grief about the same things. My study shows that very few, indeed, had the opportunity to actually work on solving some of their own problems. It was all about the child.

During the time that a program was being established for each individual child, we tried to understand what parents were feeling. We never tried to direct feelings or tell anyone how they should be feeling. We just tried to give them our best information and listen to their reaction. Some family members expressed their gratitude for this acceptance of them and their child. They said that even though they knew people were trying to be helpful, it was always a negative reaction when someone told them how they should be feeling or acting.

There appear to be several things that are strong determinants of the outcome of grief. In the past, childhood experiences may have built subconscious barriers that are hard to overcome. Experiences during the developmental years of a child may also create barriers. So many parents have related to being punished for having hostile feelings or feelings of anger. They were admonished for demonstrating their anger and frustration. It is now only normal that they should avoid such demonstrations in later years.

Previous mental illness may also be a major factor in determining how a person handles their grief. If a person has been treated for mental illness, they are less likely to express feelings that might get them into further trouble. A display of confusion or hostility might cause others to think that their mental illness was catching up with them again.

Past relations with handicapped persons will also be a factor to bring out into the open and discuss. If it was a positive relationship, so much the better. If not, then it could cause problems of rejection.

We have previously discussed the role of males and females in our society. Another factor that gets involved in dealing with handicapped children is age. Young people appear to have more options than do older folks. They have their whole life ahead of them. After all, it is often felt that older people have lived their lives and are expected to sacrifice more.

These perceptions may not be particularly right; nevertheless, it is the way our society thinks. Very few of us are able to disregard the mores of those around us.

Personality is always a factor that determines the outcome of grief. Some people are easy-going and accept hardships as an everyday occurrence. By nature of their personality, they take things in stride and go about doing what needs to be done. On the other hand, some personalities are extremely volatile. They are the screamers and wailers. They react to problems in confused and disorganized ways. Some personalities seem to have a proneness to grief. They can feel down over the least little thing. No matter what type of person you are, you have a right to be you.

Socioeconomic status also plays a major role in determining the outcome of grief. When finances are available to take care of things, it is a much easier path to follow and less stressful. Remember, stress can cause illness. When a family does not have the means to provide the best for its child, then there is another dimension to the anger and guilt. A family is indeed fortunate when it lives in a community that has provided services for handicapped children at no cost or is based on ability to pay.

Nature has a way of healing us. We have noticed that once depression has been acknowledged, parents may go through what is called "desensitization." At first everything reminds them of their pain, then as time goes by, they are only occasionally reminded. We learn desensitization so that we will not hurt so much. As a therapist, it was something that I had to learn about and work at. Even after we have gone through several stages of grief and become less sensitive, there will be unexpected occasions when grief reaches out and grabs us. After a while, we can anticipate difficult days and dates. It is helpful to plan for days like that, particularly birthdays, anniversaries, Mother's Day, Father's Day, Thanksgiving, Christmas, etc. We need to plan to keep busy and keep our minds on constructive paths.

If you resist your pain, which is a natural thing to do, you may find it is replaced by a nagging ache that is likely to take its place. A low-grade crisis may endure for years. Grief doesn't go away just because you choose to ignore it. We have discussed how we must take our grief and handle it, get through it and recoup from it. The big questions become "How do we convert all of these negative emotions into something useful?" and "How do we get on that track to recovery?" What we must do is take each stage of our grief, recognize it for what it is, and deal with it. Then, welcome the next stage and recognize it for what it is. In the end, we will come out whole.

We may establish boundaries within which we may operate. These boundaries are not set in concrete. They are like shoulders on a highway that allow an added safety feature, giving us time to get back on track should we swerve out of control. This chapter has dealt with the need to continue in our grief and handle it. If we do so, we will come out the other end a whole, healthy person. The last chapter will deal with suggestions from those parents who have lived the life and dealt with it. Their suggestions may fit your lifestyle or not, but they will give you something constructive to think about based on other people's experience.

Chapter 13

The Gift of Grief

Our grief may be one of the strongest emotions that we ever feel. It might only be less strong than love. It is an intense emotional response to our loss in life and can be devastating in that respect. More important, grief is an emotion that can be a painful, spiritual, and psychological trip through the healing process.

Typically, we do not appreciate the healing powers of grief, yet they are strong and beneficial. It is amazing as the healing occurs after a traumatic incident. Kubler-Ross and Kessler (15) say that "grief transforms the broken, wounded soul, a soul that no longer wants to get up in the morning, a soul that can find no reason for living, a soul that has suffered unbelievable loss." They go on to say that grief alone has the power to heal.

In our own study, we have seen people in all stages of the grief process. Then, we see them a year later. For those who grieved, we saw significant change in their health and their happiness. For those who did not find that happiness, we could not document their grief process. We concluded that not only does grief work, it heals. If we do not work through our grief, there is no healing of the mind, spirit, and body.

We have not been taught to grieve, and we don't teach our children how to grieve. We find teenagers in our society who have never been to a funeral. They have never been allowed to see those other people grieve. They are protected from it.

Few people discuss with their children the grief that they suffered when their parents died or were injured. They never modeled grief for their children; thus, those children missed the gift of grief.

Not having grief modeled for you and not having access to grief counselors, most people today feel very lonely in their grief. They may feel that no one understands or shares their pain. Grief models are few and far between. They often have to turn to family who are themselves unfamiliar of uncomfortable with the grieving process.

Recently, I watched NBC News and observed the grief of some people in Iraq who had suffered death in their family because of a suicide bomber. In the crowded streets, they cried, screamed, beat the ground with their fists, and in some instances beat themselves about the head. Perhaps it is true that you can only hurt in one spot at a time, and, at a time like that, physical pain was preferable.

Not knowing how to grieve, we avoid it. That does not seem to be the answer. Then, comes the question "Why bother to grieve?" Kubler-Ross and Kessler (15) give two reasons. First, those who grieve well, live well. Second, and most important, grief is a healing process of the heart, soul, and mind; it is the path that returns us to wholeness. They go on to say, "It shouldn't be a matter of if you grieve; the question is when you grieve." It has been observed in our study that if you don't grieve, you will always have unfinished business. That encompasses everything that hasn't been said or done in relation to the cause of our pain. These unfinished tasks can resurface at any time and literally "mess up" your day. Especially in grief for handicapped children, it may resurface in the middle of a new grief process that is taking place because there will be other grief processes. When it happens, it further complicates and inhibits us from making progress with the new grief.

Grief is a gift we all experience. It equalizes our experiences. People around us do not know how to help. They may want to, but they don't know what that help would be. They don't know what you need.

I read a story in Reader's Digest, years ago, that told a story of how a man had reached out to help a family. They had received word that a father had died, and they were going to travel across country to attend the funeral. In the midst of gathering together all that was needed for the trip, there was a knock at the door. Their neighbor stood on the porch, shoe shine kit in hand. He said simply, "I'm here to shine shoes." They were astounded. That was something that they hadn't considered. So, while they prepared for their trip, the neighbor sat quietly in the kitchen and shined everyone's shoes. It was a gesture that they never forgot.

Some people are hesitant to share our grief because it reminds them of their own pain. In reality, we will all grieve forever. You learn to live with it. Some grief is mild, and some is severe. But, if you don't do it, you will never be whole again. If you do, you have received a great gift.

The other day, I experienced a grief process. It came and went very quickly, but I recognized the pattern of it and laughed within a minute after the incident happened. What was the incident that brought the grief process? Well, I was wearing a brand-new shirt, and as I went through a gate in the backyard, I snagged a nail and tore the sleeve. My first response was "What the heck?" (shock) "I can't believe I did that." (denial) "Damn, damn, damn." (anger) "I should have been more careful." (guilt) "Oh well, I have to buy a new shirt." (acceptance and reestablishment) I had in effect gone through the complete grief process in about one minute. All I can say at this point is "Man, I have a good life going." Putting that aside, I do have incidents in my life that caused grief. I had bone cancer as a small child. I suffered a failed marriage and missed participating in the teen years of my three sons. I have had other injuries and disappointments, but I received the gift of grief and came out whole. You can too, if you let it happen.

Chapter 14

Suggestions for Parents

Realistically, grief is an excruciating, painful emotion. People who are psychologically healthy generally do blame themselves and agonize over situations of genuine negligence. Until they have worked out in their minds just what happened, these emotions are with them in their state of doubt. In a significant loss, this process has usually taken six months to a year to work through. At that point, healing may have taken place, but as in all wounds, a scar will remain.

It is normal to devote one's self to the ill, forgetting the normal folks who are around. It is normal for siblings to resent the attention that the disabled child receives. They will grieve the loss of their parent's attention.

With these thoughts in mind, I set forth and talked to parents and professional people to find out what works and what doesn't. From those discussions I have come up with some "do" and "don't" scenarios to make parents' adjustments a little easier and more helpful.

First, remember: It is natural to agonize over that excruciating, painful emotion that comes with grief. It is natural to be self-centered at a time like this. It is natural to attempt to devote one's self to the handicapped child to the exclusion of all others. Jealousy on the part of the spouse or siblings is normal. It is natural to search for what is lost. "If only" becomes a big part of the language of mourning. Some may feel a need for atonement (a respectable period of mourning).

Some parents turn to self-preoccupation as a way to rebuild their lives. When people enter the stage of rebuilding their lives, they are in danger of getting carried away.

Second, authors who have studied grief generally agree: Changes in schedules produce anger. You will definitely be faced with changes in schedules due to the needs of your new child. These changes are not going to be temporary. There will be needs that must be met in terms of therapy, medical treatments, and education. We have on record children who have had as many as twenty-three surgeries during their first three years of life.

Too much change can be troublesome. Therefore, we need to keep things as stable as possible. Change schedules when necessary, but keep things in place when possible such as meals, school, bedtime, etc.

After determining a course, communicate with those around you. It will soften the blow to their life if they know what is going on and what to expect. When their life is more stable, your life is more stable.

It is helpful to have a neutral observer. We found that those who had friends involved were able to use the feedback that they received to help stabilize the environment.

It is helpful to maintain communication with the other children in the family. If we tell them about the new child's problems and then drop them, it solves nothing. Keep them in the loop all the way. If you do, they will probably keep that contact with their sibling long after you are gone.

Children understand more than we give them credit for. Never underestimate the ability of a child to understand the problem and your feelings about the problem and to have the ability to adjust. Kids are very flexible. A friend of mine related an experience that brought this home. He's old like me and bald-headed, like me. As he sat in the waiting room at a children's hospital where his grandson was receiving treatment, a little girl, about four years old, came by. She stopped by his side and reached up to take his hand. "Is that a chemo-cut?" she asked. "No," he said. "I'm just getting old and bald." She patted his hand and said, "That's good," and went on down the hall. How sad that a child that age has to face those problems in life. But, she had, and she was concerned with others. She understood.

Some families want to move out when handicapped children enter the family. Whether it is from embarrassment or just feeling that they need a new start because their life has changed, we don't always know. It is just something that they often think about. When they do move, they have left part of their support group behind. Good friends and neighbors are important to the recovery process. The only good reason to move is to go where there are services available to your child that are not available where you presently live.

Parents in grief often overlook the obvious. A comfortable environment, good friends, and old haunts are very comforting. Hang on to them.

Personal growth is important at a time like this. Learn all you can about your child's problems and condition. Learn all you can about the services that are available in your community and your state. Personal growth is also important and a must at a time that your ego has taken a beating.

Get back into your routines as quickly as possible. It is the new and unknown that tend to upset our lives. Get back into that comfortable routine that you are familiar with just as soon as you can. Familiar and comfort go together.

Go out of the way to maintain a social and emotional atmosphere that is consistent with your past life. Good friends are hard to beat at a time like this. They may hold back at first because they don't know how to help. Pull them back in and just let them be themselves.

Very important: write down your angers and your fears on paper. It not only helps to get it out; it helps to review occasionally to see if those angers were justified in the light of a new day. And, did those fears really come forward to ruin your life as you expected?

Work at keeping your child presentable. Style their hair, teach them to be clean, wipe their noses, and stand tall. It will make their life so much better. While working in a school system, back in the 1960s, I was involved in getting special education classes out of the "old buildings" and integrated into the regular school system. In those days, it was customary to have all of the special education classes on one campus. Usually it was a campus that had been abandoned, then reopened for special education. We had a class assigned to enter a school that had a principal who had argued against such a move. With doubt in my mind, I went by to visit and see if there was anything I could do to make the transition easier. To my surprise, I was met at the front door with a handshake and a pat on the back. The principal said, "I'm so glad you're here. I have a couple of requests to make." I thought, "Oh boy, here it comes." The principal's request was truly remarkable. He had total concern and sympathy for the kids. What his request was this: hairstyling for the girls, getting rid of those "retarded haircuts" on the boys, and teaching them "not to walk retarded." He said, "You can spot those kids a block away." Talk about curriculum change! The results were fantastic and became a model for the whole city. The change in attitude, appearance, and academic skills was great. As we often hear down here in Texas, "He done good." I included this last story to make the point that there is a need to help our children be attractive. It not only makes them more acceptable to those that they meet in public, it helps to build their self-esteem. I have truly witnessed the results of these "makeovers" on handicapped children, and it is always favorable. Never have I seen it fail to be of great benefit to that child.

Throughout this book, I have repeatedly referred to "handicapped children." Over the years the terms have changed, usually as a perception that it is a less derogatory term. We have gone from "handicapped" to "disabled" to "special needs" children. There is nothing derogatory about being handicapped, disabled, or in need of special treatment. It is a fact of life that we must deal with. Perhaps I have stuck with the term handicapped because it was most used during my years in the field. Perhaps it was because that was the term used at a time I discovered the grief of the parents involved with our program. Call it what you may but get the help you need to provide for yourself and your family as you deal with the needs of your "special" child.

There is one more thing I would ask you to do. I have included a personal note at the end of this book. Please take time to read it. It explains my feelings.

A Personal Note

Working with handicapped children has been my pleasure and my occupation. It is a large part of my life. It is a time that I soar with the eagles, feel the adrenaline flow through my veins, and know that I am really alive. It is a time that I reach out and touch the face of God. It is a time of happiness and exhilaration and a time of peace and contentment.

Then, I am brought crashing back to earth by the reality of the life of my "kids." They may be happy or unhappy. They may be treatable or untreatable. They may be hopeful or hopeless. One thing is for sure, however, they are real, and their families are real.

I do not have handicapped children of my own. I have had over four thousand children with disabilities and their families during the last forty-one years. Averaging four members per family, that means I have had sixteen thousand family members, all of whom I consider my own.

Families of kids with disabilities, by nature, put up a good front. They smile, do the right things, and take care of their own. I commend them for that. But, their strength and caring did not communicate to me the grief that they suffered. It was years before I met a big, strong, courageous man who let the tears flow and told me, "I hurt so bad I can't stand the pain." His open, honest confession caused me to reach out and ask others about their grief. Believe me, I was astounded.

I wish I could hug each and every parent of a child with disabilities and tell them, "Everything's going to be alright."

Ben

Bibliography

1. Anderson, C., Aspects of Pathological Grief and Mourning, Introduction to Psycho-Analysis 30:48, 1949
2. Davidson, Rusty L., In The Hands of God, Fairfax, VA: Xulon Press, 2006
3. Fleishman, Alan R., M.D., The Immediate Impact of the Birth of a Low Birth Weight Infant on the Family, Bulletin of the National Center for Clinical Infant Programs, Vol. VI. No. 4, April, 1986
4. Fried, M., Grieving for a Lost Home, New York Basic Books, 1962
5. Gorer, G., Death, Grief and Mourning in Contemporary Britain, London: Cresset, 1965
6. Jeffreys, J. Shep, Helping Grieving People: When Tears Are Not Enough, New York: Brunner-Routledge, 2005
7. Jenkins, Clare & Merry, Judy, Relative Grief, Philadelphia, P.A.: Jessica Kingsley Publishers, 2005
8. Kavanaugh, Robert E., Facing Death, Los Angeles, C.A.: Nash Publishing, 1972
9. Krumroy, Jeri, Grief is Not Forever, Brethren Press, 1985
10. Kubler-Ross, Elizabeth, M.D. Death, The Final Stage of Growth, Englewood Cliffs, N.J.: Prentice-Hall, Inc.
11. Kubler-Ross, Elizabeth, M.D. Living With Death and Dying, New York: MacMillan Publishing Co. Inc., 1981
12. Kubler-Ross, Elizabeth, M.D., On Children and Death, New York: MacMillan Publishing Co. Inc., 1983
13. Kubler-Ross, Elizabeth, M.D., Questions and Answers on Death and Dying, New York: Simon & Schuster, 1997

14. Kubler-Ross, Elizabeth, M.D., On Death and Dying, New York: MacMillan Publishing Co. Inc., 1997 & 2003

15. Kubler-Ross, Elizabeth, M.D., & Kessler, David, On Grief and Grieving, New York: Scribner, 2007

16. McDonald, Eugene T., Understanding Those Feelings, Pittsburgh, P.A.: Stanwix House, Inc., 1962

17. Oates, Wayne E., Your Particular Grief, Philadelphia, P.A.: Westminster Press,

18. Olshansky, Simon, Chronic Sorrow: A Response To Having A Mentally Retarded Child, Social Casework, Vol. XLIII, No. 4, April, 1962

19. Parks, Colin & Murray, Bereavement-Studies Of Grief In Adult Life, New York: International Universities Press, Inc.,1972

20. Parks, Ronda M., Parental Reactions to the Birth of a Handicapped Child, Health and Social Work, Vol. 2, No. 3, August, 1977

21. Stearns, Ann Kaiser, Living Through Personal Crisis, New York: Ballantine Books, 1984

22. Veisson, Saar & Magi, Depression Among Parents with a Mentally Retarded Child, London, UK: MacKeith & Dale, 1973

23. Westberg, Granger E., Good Grief, Minneapolis, MN: Fortress Press, 1997

24. Wolfelt, Alan D., Healing Your Grieving Heart, Fort Collins, CO: Companion Press, 2001

25. Worden, J. William, Grief Counseling and Grief Therapy, New York: Springer Publishing Co., 2002

26. Youngs, Robert, Layman's Movement for a Christian World.

Get Published, Inc!
Thorofare, NJ 08086
31 August 2009
BA2009243